# *A Miracle for Michael*

The doctor stepped over to Karen and with a joyous smile said, "Karen, I don't profess to know how or why this has happened. I've heard about you and your friends praying every night for Michael. Maybe that's it. But one thing is certain—your son is showing signs of a remarkable recovery from his coma. If I'm right, and the medication I just ordered works like I believe it will, Michael should be waking up within forty-five minutes."

The following forty-five minutes were the longest in Karen's life. As the minutes passed, the room began to fill with doctors and nurses. When Karen lowered her head and began to repeat the Lord's Prayer, every person there joined with her.

Just minutes after the prayer was finished, young Michael opened his eyes for the first time in more than a month . . . and spoke . . .

"Hi, Mom. Why are you crying?"

*Other Avon Books by*
**James Pruitt**

ANGELS BESIDE YOU
THE COMPLETE ANGEL

# HEALED BY PRAYER

JAMES PRUITT

AVON BOOKS NEW YORK

AVON BOOKS, INC.
1350 Avenue of the Americas
New York, New York 10019


Published by arrangement with the author
Library of Congress Catalog Card Number: 99-94454
ISBN: 0-380-79758-5
**www.avonbooks.com**



First Avon Books Printing: November 1999



Printed in the U.S.A.

WCD 10 9 8 7 6 5 4 3 2 1

# ACKNOWLEDGMENTS

There are a number of people I wish to thank for their support as I was writing this book.

First, my friend Tom Colgan, who has always been there for me when things have gotten a little rocky.

Tia Maggini, my editor at Avon Books, who kept me on the right track whenever I began to wander into the byways of self-righteousness.

Of course, all you wonderful people who wrote in answer to my ads in newspapers, magazines, and church bulletins. Without you, there would not have been a book. Thank you so much.

A big thank-you to the folks at the *Daily Word* in Unity Village, Missouri. Your kindness provided not only assistance, but renewed faith in myself as well.

And last, but not least, Charlotte, my loving wife of twenty-eight years, who went to bed alone many a night with the sound of typewriter keys echoing through the house. I am grateful to God for many things in my life, but God gave me the greatest gift when he provided me with this woman who has shared her life with me. Through good times and bad, there have been two things in my life I have never doubted—my Lord God and my wife, Charlotte.

# CONTENTS

# HEALED BY PRAYER

# PROLOGUE

*Prayer:* a reverent petition made to God or another deity. An act of communion with God.

*Miracle:* an event that appears unexplainable by the laws of nature and therefore is held to be supernatural in origin or an act of God.

In a small community church in rural Kentucky, a minister and his congregation of fifteen pray to God with near-hysterical abandon to perform a miracle for one of their own who is dying of cancer.

A congregation numbering nearly a thousand in a Chicago church unite in a moment of silent prayer for a member of their church who has lost a loved one.

All across this country and around the world, people of every race and religion are calling upon God for one reason or another.

Imagine, if you can, what would happen if we could place a satellite in orbit around the earth that monitored nothing but prayers.

What would be the average count per day? What kind of prayers would be made?

Just how powerful is this thing called prayer? And can prayer actually produce miracles?

For most of recorded civilization, men and women have fervently believed in the power of prayer and the miracles that it could effect. They trusted that a strong belief and powerful faith were all they needed to evoke an act of intervention from a higher power in their lives.

Today more and more of us are in search of greater spiritual fulfillment. We have rediscovered the power of prayer and with that power belief in acts of divine intervention—intervention so powerful as to be called a miracle.

# INTRODUCTION

The idea for this book came about following a conversation I had with an elderly member of our church.

It was a beautiful April Sunday. My wife and I had arrived at the church early that morning, she to teach Sunday school and I to attend a meeting to discuss the cost of building an addition onto our church for a day care center.

After my meeting had finished, I went to our usual pew to wait for my wife. As I was glancing over the program for the day's service, Emma Teal, a delightful woman seventy years young, introduced me to her sister, who was visiting from Kansas City.

Emma's sister was carrying a copy of a book I had written about angels, and she asked me if I would mind signing it. Of course, I was more than happy to. As we discussed the book, Emma's sister, Hanna, bought up the subject of healing evangelists and the healing power of prayer. I could tell that Emma was uncomfortable with this subject, but before she could pull her sister away, Hanna began to tell me about a faith-healing revival she had attended in Kansas City and of all the miraculous things she had witnessed. Emma could only sit quietly and shake her head.

Then Hanna asked me, "Mr. Pruitt, you've written two books about angels. So you must believe in them. Why haven't you written a book about the wonderful healing power of faith and prayer? You believe in that too, don't you?"

I must admit the question took me by surprise, and I didn't know how to reply. Visions of television evangelists flashed through my mind, as did the movie *Elmer Gantry*, with Burt Lancaster thumping his Bible while delivering a hellfire and brimstone sermon, and my grandmother, God bless her, who never missed an Oral Roberts program for as long as I can remember.

I never did give Hanna an answer, but her question remained with me for days. I told my wife about it, and her reply was a simple one: "If you believe it, then fine. But if you have doubts, then find out. Remember, you had doubts about angels as well."

But there is a big difference between healing prayer and angels. Encounters with angels, which include visions, a gentle touch, or a voice, are usually experienced by one or two people. Prayer, on the other hand, especially prayer that actually heals or cures an individual, involves a great number of people: the patient, family members, doctors, hospital staff, clergy, and often a congregation of hundreds—even thousands—that witness this healing miracle.

In the course of a religious upbringing, I was taught the stories of the Bible at an early age—stories of how Jesus had healed the sick, made the blind see, and made the lame walk. But once you move past the Bible, what then? Did the miracles stop after Jesus left this earth? If not, then who carried them on and when? The disciples were said to have carried on Jesus' healing ways. Do miracle healers exist in today's world?

Are there still miracles of healing going on? And are they the direct result of prayer?

Before I began writing about angels, I had been a little skeptical about their existence. But now, having written two books on the subject and read countless others, I can assure you that I firmly believe in angels. I must admit that I began this project the same way—a little skeptical about what I was going to find once I began to probe into the subject of healing prayer. I hoped the result would be as joyous as my acceptance of angels, so I decided to accept dear, sweet Hanna's challenge.

The results of my personal interviews and research are here for you to read and evaluate. I hope that you will find them as uplifting and wonderful as I do.

# PRAYER

Just what do people pray for?

According to a *Newsweek* poll, 82 percent pray for the health or success of a family member, 75 percent pray for the strength to overcome a personal weakness.

Now, I am not a professional gambler by any means, but I must confess to a weakness whenever football season rolls around. There are certain teams that I like more than others, and I have a tendency to allow that admiration (along with my big mouth) to force me into situations in which a wager is necessary to uphold the honor of my favorite team. Having already shown a total lack of willpower by making the wager, I then find myself on the edge of my chair on Sunday afternoon, invoking the name of God more times than I care to mention here. But all the men (and women, these days) who have ever wagered on a football game, I can assure you, have called upon a higher power more than once. Especially when the stakes are high, there is only one minute left to play, and their team is behind. It is in that final minute of every football game that God and Heaven are literally bombarded with a barrage of prayers from supporters of both teams. Now, the question is: Does God answer those prayers?

Of thirteen hundred people polled, 61 percent stated that they firmly believed God would never answer a prayer involving a sports event. (Now, that one I can personally attest to!)

When asked, "Does God often play favorites?" an amazing 83 percent responded that there was no way that God would ever play favorites.

In today's troubled times, these numbers are good news. Look around you. Have you noticed the doubts that people have about practically everything? You can almost feel the cynicism in the air around us. If you think I may be exaggerating, just listen the next time you hear someone talking about members of the Congress or Senate. These men and women are the chosen leaders of our country. When they appear on television or radio and profess that they are doing great things in Washington for us, the people, pause a moment and listen to what those around you say. Look at their faces when they speak. More than likely, what you will see will be a smirk followed by the words, "Yeah, right! They're all crooks."

We have grown skeptical about everything and everybody—not only politics, but our jobs and our futures as well. But who can blame us? There was a time when a person could work for the same company, factory, or business for twenty-five years and be rewarded for his steadfast loyalty and dedication. But those days are gone. In today's high-speed world of computers and automation, no one's job is one hundred percent safe, and we know it.

Yet with all the worry, stress, and skepticism that plagues us, our trust and belief in God continues. He is not going to downsize us, tell us that we are too young and have no experience or that we are too old. Like a rock in a swirling, often angry sea, he is always there for us to talk to whenever we want. We have only to call his name.

Can you possibly imagine what it must be like to receive all the prayers that rise toward Heaven every minute of every day, prayers for the ill and the dying, prayers for pets, for success, for love and peace throughout the world? How can God possibly answer this multitude of prayers all coming to him at once?

Dorothy Reece, who runs a prayer line in her Roman Catholic parish in Newton, Massachusetts, says, "God has the ability to take care of more than one person at a time." As many as fifty members of her congregation pray with those who call the prayer line. Her prayer registry is constantly filled with requests for prayers dealing with everything from medical emergencies and substance abuse to job interviews.

This only supports what the *Newsweek* poll revealed. More and more people are coming back to prayer and invoking the help of the Lord. We may have become a more cynical people, but we have not become so cynical as to have lost our faith in God.

Just as there are all types of people, there are many ways to pray. Each of us is unique, and each has his or her own way of praying, of asking God to come into our hearts and give us peace.

For true believers, there is no question that God hears their prayers. For them, no proof of miracles is required. They are at peace with themselves and their God. They know that healing prayer is an attainable, life-changing force. The healing love of God is in their lives, and because of this they can experience a new freedom. They learn to forgive and ask for forgiveness with greater courage, becoming more aware of their weakness and limitations. They develop a greater sensitivity to the needs of family, friends, and acquaintances.

For those who doubt, who believe that prayer is no more than pure folly, no proof or miracle, short of a face-to-face confrontation with God himself, could ever change their mind.

I often think what a pity that is. For those people who doubt, life must be a daily hell all its own, although they would never admit it. Imagine living each day surrounded by uncertainty, tension, doubt, and stress in this world besieged by drugs and alcohol and violence and war.

Who do they turn to for reassurance? Who do they cry out to for inner peace? Who is there for them when all others have no time for them?

What a terrible and lonely place this world must be without God.

# THE PHYSICIAN

*Hold the physician in honor, for he is essential to you, and God it was who established his profession.*

*From God the physician has his wisdom, and the king provides for his sustenance.*

*His knowledge makes the physician distinguished, and gives him access to those in authority.*

*God makes the earth yield healing herbs which the prudent man should not neglect; was not the water sweetened by a twig that men might learn his power?*

*He endows men with the knowledge to glory in his mighty works, through which the physician eases pain and the druggist prepares his medicines; thus God's creative work continues without cease in its efficacy on the surface of the earth.*

*My son, when you are ill, delay not, but pray to God, who will heal you; offer your sweet-smelling ablation and petition, a rich offering according to your means. Then give the physician his place lest he leave; for you need him too.*

*There are times that give him an advantage, and he too beseeches God; that his diagnosis may be correct and his treatment bring about a cure.*

*He who is a sinner toward his Maker will be defiant toward the physician.*

—JESUS BEN SIRA, *Ecclesiasticus*, 38: 1–15*

This passage, written during the second century B.C., when medicine was in its infancy, clearly shows the relationship between God and the physician. It reminds the reader of the power of prayer while recognizing that God also works through the skills and medicines of the physician to cure the afflicted.

Dr. Elmer Hess, former president of the American Medical Association and a specialist in urology, made the following remarks at the forty-eighth annual meeting of the Southern Medical Association, which ranked second to the American Medical Association as the largest general medical organization in the country. "A physician who walks into a sick room is not alone. He can only minister to the ailing person with the material tools of scientific

*The entire Book of Ecclesiasticus is not in many Protestant versions of the Bible, but it is only listed among the Apocrypha. This quotation is from *The New American Bible* translation.

medicine. His faith in a higher power does the rest. Show me the doctor who denies the existence of the Supreme Being, and I will say that he has no right to practice the healing art.

"Our medical schools are doing a magnificent job of teaching the fundamentals of scientific medicine; however, I'm afraid that the concentration on basic science is so great that the teaching of spiritual values is all but neglected."

Although his words might have seemed rather harsh to medical professionals in 1932, it is quite obvious that Dr. Hess firmly believed in the power of divine healing working in partnership with the physician.

Was Dr. Hess's opinion correct? A doctor can diagnose, and he can prescribe a variety of medications. He can provide his patient with the best services that medical science has to offer. But in the final analysis, isn't it God who heals through his divine power?

The doctor possesses the power and skill to set and repair broken bones, but once he has done everything possible within the limits of his talents, he still must wait for divine power to complete the healing process.

Likewise, a skilled surgeon who is a master with the scalpel can utilize all his God-given talents to perform the most difficult operations on his patients; yet when the operation is complete, the physician, confident that he has done all that is humanly possible for his patient, must resign himself to wait for a higher power to do the actual healing. He waits for nature (God) to heal gradually.

There are those who set doctors and believers in the healing power of prayer against one another. But Dr. Hess realized years ago that they needed each other. The doctors, the nurses, and the faith healers all need to come together to form a team working toward one major goal: healing the afflicted.

Unfortunately, this has not always been the case. In fact, there was a time when the medical profession saw all faith healers as con men and charlatans, and in some cases it was right. But not all of them were the reckless, irresponsible phonies they were accused of being. Some actually performed miraculous feats of healing that defied explanation by some of the finest and most respected members of the medical community.

If Dr. Hess were to address the Medical Association today, I believe he would find he would have to rewrite his fiery speech. Today many in the medical profession are convinced that prayers and a strong faith can significantly improve a patient's chances of recovery, and several of them around the country are trying to test prayer's effectiveness in healing.

Now, I know that if you are a true believer, the word "test" jumped right out at you as you were reading. Please keep in mind what I mentioned at the beginning of this book. There are millions that believe, but there is also a considerable number that does not. Skeptics and cynics must be shown. Remember, for the believer, no proof is necessary. For those who doubt, no proof will be sufficient.

There are now teams of dedicated doctors in many parts of the country determined to find proof that satisfies not only themselves, but nonbelievers as well. But will their proofs be sufficient for nonbelievers? Who can say. One thing I am certain of: They will have a strong ally watching over them.

At the time this book was being written, a number of these tests were in the works. One such test was conducted in Clearwater, Florida, under the direction of Dr. Dale Matthews, an associate professor of medicine at the Georgetown University School of Medicine in Washington, D.C.

Dr. Matthews, a Presbyterian who has been praying for and with his patients for years, took on no easy task in trying to find out if science can confirm once and for all the healing power of prayer.

The patients under Dr. Matthews's study consisted of sixty subjects from the Arthritis Treatment Center all suffering from rheumatoid arthritis, a painful, crippling disease that swells the joints, particularly joints of the fingers, hands, arms, and legs. For those afflicted with this disease, the simple act of pouring a glass of water or spreading butter on a piece of bread can be an ordeal of pure torture.

The swelling and pain that accompany this form of arthritis are clearly perceptible. That is exactly why Dr. Matthews selected this disease for his test. Relief of these symptoms will be obvious and can be easily measured.

The patients were divided into two groups. All the patients received four days of healing prayer provided by members of the Christian Healing Ministry through the traditional Christian practice of laying on of hands. One group received in addition six months of long-distance prayer. Both groups were examined by the same doctor before the experiment, immediately after, and again after one, three, six, and twelve months.

Acutely aware of the scrutiny given his study by both skeptics and believers alike, Dr. Matthews abided by the strict scientific standards and protocol established by the American College of Rheumatology. The material and data gathered by Dr. Matthews and his dedicated team were evaluated by a physician not associated with the research.

By March 1997, early into the study, some members of the group had already shown extraordinary signs of short-term results. One male patient began the study with forty-nine tender joints. After four sessions with a hands-on prayer minister, he had only eight tender joints, and there was visible reduction of swelling in a number of areas. Six months later he had none and no longer needed his medication.

Will all of the patients in the study do as well? Only time will tell. In the meantime, Dr. Matthews continues his work alongside the Great Physician.

"I think this is a historic time," he says. "The spiritual traditions of healing will be joined with surgery and pharmaceuticals. I think we're entering the era of prayer and Prozac."

In December of 1996, another well-known physician, Dr. Herbert Benson, a Harvard Medical School cardiologist and founder of the Mind-Body Institute at Beth Israel Deaconess Hospital, attended a seminar at Harvard. The subject was Spirituality and Healing in Medicine. Upon his arrival, Dr. Benson was quoted in the Boston paper: "I'm not a religious person. I came to this meeting, not from belief, but from science. Honestly, I came to this meeting with feet dragging."

Not long after this seminar, *Maclean's* magazine reported that Dr. Benson and other scientists had confirmed what many theologians had long believed: that prayer and other types of meditative breaks during the day could have astounding therapeutic effects.

According to Dr. Benson, studies had found that two ten-minute prayer sessions per day could lower the heart rate, slow breathing, and quiet brain wave activity. They also showed that prayer or meditation could avert the need for invasive surgery and substantially reduce the need for visits to a doctor. Furthermore, an amazing 35 percent of couples who believed themselves to be infertile conceived within six months of beginning prayer or meditation and chronic pain sufferers reported substantial relief, as did those enduring the symptoms of cancer and AIDS.

Dr. David Larson, M.D., is President of the National Institute for Healthcare Research in Rockville, Maryland. He has been studying and compiling information on the relationship between medicine and healing prayer for more than twenty years and has found that the majority of all studies of the role of religion in health care have proven that the more people pray, the less prone they are to mental and physical illness.

Studies by the Institute have shown that among churchgoers, the death rate from coronary artery disease is 50 percent lower and the suicide rate 53 percent lower than among people who do not attend religious services. They have also found that a strong sense of faith and prayer can help reduce the effects of stress and is directly associated with decreased recovery time after major surgery.

At Dartmouth-Hitchcock Medical Center in New Hampshire, a study of 232 patients undergoing coronary bypass surgery found that strength and comfort gained from a powerful religious faith was the single most consistent predictor of survival. The more religious the patient, the greater the protective effect. Of the 232 patients involved, 195 stated that they were either fairly religious, slightly religious, or not religious at all. Of these, twenty-one died within six months of their surgery. The thirty-seven patients who professed strong and deeply seated religious faith have all survived and are doing well today.

So what does this tell us? Some scientists will scoff and loudly proclaim that this does not prove a thing. Undoubtedly these people would have a lot of supporters. But one thing is certain: There are thirty-seven people who would just as quickly step forward as living proof that the skeptics are wrong.

The most meaningful results of these various studies have been the effect that their results have had on today's medical community. The indisputable link between a patient's faith and the healing process has stirred the interest of today's doctors. In fact, a survey conducted by the American Academy of Family Physicians found that 99 percent of doctors believe that there is an important connection between the spirit and the body.

These findings may be news to the medical community, but not to the thousands of believers who have witnessed the power of prayer and faith in their lives.

There are those who still classify remarkable cases of healing as unexplainable events or consequence of incorrect diagnosis. Before I began this book, I could have been included in this group. But my research and personal interviews with people who have actually experienced a divine healing quickly brought me over to the side of the believers.

I leave these stories for you to read and come to your own conclusions. When you have finished this book, I believe you will feel, as I do, that the power of prayer, linked with an unwavering faith, can produce miracles.

## A BAPTIST CONVERSION

Robert Charles Colson was sixty years old in 1979, a dedicated Baptist from Macon, Georgia. A cabinet builder by trade, Robert took pride in his work, a state of mind passed down by his father. "A man who has no pride in his craft has even less in himself" were his father's favorite words. It was a motto Robert adhered to in honor of his father.

It was that hardworking spirit that endeared Robert to his family and friends. He was a caring father, a faithful husband, and a good friend to all who knew him. He had grown up in the small towns and rural areas of Georgia. Robert was ten years old when the Depression wiped out his father's business. Like so many other Americans of the time, they found themselves on the road, moving from town to town so that his father might find work. Sometimes the work lasted for only a few days. When they were lucky, they got to stay an entire month in one place.

Those were the lean years for the Colsons. But no matter how tough things got, Robert's parents would never end the day without a prayer. Money may have been in short supply, but religion, faith, and perseverance were never lacking in the Colson family. Bible reading became Robert's only form of entertainment.

There was no television in those days. The family couldn't afford a radio and only occasionally spent their hard-earned money on a newspaper. That left the Bible as the prime source of reading material, which suited Robert's mother, a staunch Baptist herself, just fine. By the time he was nineteen, Robert had read the huge family Bible from cover to cover no less than seven times. (Now, if you don't think that's very many times, I suggest you try it once.)

In early 1941, the Colsons found themselves in Macon, Georgia. Robert's father had impressed a well-to-do furniture manufacturer with his skillful work and attention to detail. Before long, the elder Colson was the foreman of the plant.

Then came the war, and Robert was drafted. At the train station, his mother and father presented him with a small, abbreviated version of the Bible and reminded him to turn to it whenever he felt his faith waver. They were confident it would protect their son from the horrors of war. They were right. Robert survived and returned home with only a minor wound received in the closing days of the battle for Berlin.

While he had been away, Robert's father had started his own business; he was once again a cabinet maker. Robert joined him. By the end of 1945, Colson and Son Cabinet Builders was well known throughout Georgia. Those were the happy years, with Robert and his father working side by side.

At age thirty, he met the woman of his dreams, and they were soon married. Robert and his father built their first house with their own hands. Then came children, much to the delight of the grandparents. But joy was short-lived. In 1951, Robert's father died. Less than five years later, his mother passed away as well.

Robert continued to build the business his father had left him, and he and his family became highly active members of the local Baptist church. By the 1970s, his business had grown considerably, and he had a number of people working for him. Most were Baptist, but there were some members of the Pentecostal church as well. Of course, to Robert, a person's religious belief had absolutely nothing to do with how well he did his job. But this particular mix certainly did lead to some rather lively lunchtime discussions about prayer, miracles, and the Bible.

Many Southern Baptists believed that miracles had ended with the passing of the biblical apostles. So strong was this theological view at Robert's church that they looked with some suspicion and distrust upon other Christians who still considered God in the miracle business, especially the Pentecostals, who always seemed to be proclaiming a miracle of some type or other.

One man who enjoyed verbal duels with Robert was his friend Ray Dunn, the shop foreman and a member of the board of the Pentecostal church. Both men were experts in the Bible and would amaze those around them with their countless quotes from the Good Book, including chapter and verse, all word for word. This little game was always carried out with good humor, everyone going back to work certain that there had been no lunchtime conversions and declaring the noontime services a draw.

For Robert, the humor ended on a warm day in June of 1979. Feeling exceptionally tired and run down, he went to his family doctor for some tests. The results that came back were totally unexpected. Robert had cancer. It had gone undetected for so long that by the time it was discovered, it had invaded a kidney, a lung, and his bones. A tissue biopsy confirmed the diagnosis. Surgery alone wasn't going to do the job. The cancer had spread so quickly that marrow drawn from any bone in Robert's body would prove malignant.

In the days that followed, Robert's doctor called in a group of specialists, and they conferred on how best to prolong Robert Colson's life. But there seemed to be little hope. His wife and family were devastated by the news, as were his friends and employees. Flowers flooded his hospital room. Along with get-well cards, there were a number of handwritten prayers for his recovery.

By the end of the week, Robert's spirits dropped, and he fell into a state of deep depression. It was as if all was lost and there was nothing Robert, the doctors, or anyone else could do to change the fact that he was dying.

"It's over," he said quietly one night.

Hearing this, his wife left the hospital and returned a short time later with the small, faded, and weather-worn Bible that Robert's parents had given him when he headed off for war in 1941. Placing it in his hands, she kissed her husband gently on the forehead and whispered, "Ask him if it's over." Then she went away again, leaving Robert alone with his Bible.

Later that same evening, Ray Dunn came by to check on his friend and boss. On seeing Ray enter the room, Robert beamed a wide smile. Oblivious to all the tubes and machines around him, Robert waved his friend closer with one hand while gently rubbing his faded Bible with the other.

As Ray moved closer, he was surprised to find his old friend in such good spirits. Everyone he had talked to earlier had said that Robert was terribly depressed. But this certainly didn't appear to be a depressed man—not with a confident smile like that. Ray moved to the side of the bed.

"How are you doing, Robert?" he asked.

"Ray," he said with a smile, "it's going to be all right. I was praying and reading the Good Book when God spoke to me. He told me he was going to heal me, Ray."

Robert could tell by the look on his friend's face that Ray figured he must be high on painkillers.

"Well, now, why do you look so surprised?" he asked, with a grin. "I thought you Pentecostals had things like this happen all the time."

Ray was still a little stunned by Robert's calm disclosure that God had promised to heal him. Without thinking, he stammered, "But . . . But Robert—you're a Baptist!"

There was a moment of awkward silence, then both men broke out into laughter. By the time Ray left that evening, Robert's spirits were soaring. The two men had clasped hands and prayed together.

Over the next few days, as the doctors continued to run their tests and ponder a course of action, Robert's church and Ray's church established a prayer circle that spread beyond the confines of Macon to the entire state of Georgia.

By the end of the second week, an amazing series of events happened in rapid succession.

In the lab, a technician passing slides containing Robert's biopsy samples under a microscope was shocked to see them turn benign before his very eyes. One after another they changed. One second the cancer was obvious—the next it was gone. To make certain he was seeing what he thought he was seeing, the technician called the pathologist over to view the remaining five slides. The same thing happened. The cancer simply vanished before the pathologist's eyes. Picking up the phone, the baffled scientist called Robert's team of doctors told them what had happened, and reported that there were no signs of cancer on any of the slides for Robert Colson. He couldn't explain it, but there it was. No cancer.

In the conference room, the X rays taken on the day Robert came into the hospital hung on a set of viewer screens. These X rays showed a tumor in the kidney area. It was this tumor that was thought to be the source of the spreading cancer. But a second set, taken only an hour before the pathologist called, showed no sign of that tumor.

"What in the world is going on here?" asked the doctors. A bone marrow test was ordered immediately. The result was negative. Robert had the healthiest bone marrow they had ever seen.

Totally at a loss to explain any of this, Robert's doctors rushed their findings to a hospital in Atlanta for confirmation. They wondered if they had missed something or if all of them had misdiagnosed the case—which seemed highly unlikely—or if the cancer was still lurking somewhere else undetected by them. But the results were the same at the other hospital. There were absolutely no signs of cancer anywhere in Robert Colson's body. Neither hospital could give an explanation for this strange turn of events.

Of course, none of this seemed strange at all to Robert Colson and Ray Dunn. On a warm night in June of 1979, a man of strong and unyielding faith spoke to God and was provided an answer to his prayer. Another man organized an army of Christians to reinforce his friend's prayer. Together they orchestrated a miracle granted by God.

Robert Colson died quietly in his sleep on January 3, 1997. In the eighteen years following his recovery, no trace of cancer was ever found. It was as if it had never existed.

Robert remained forever a Baptist. But he became an outspoken advocate for belief in miracles through prayer and a fervent proponent for a change in theology at the Baptist conventions held each year.

In his will, and with the approval of his family, Robert passed the well-worn Bible of his youth to his longtime friend Ray Dunn, who would always remind people, "It wasn't me who converted Robert. It was God."

Robert [illegible] Baptist, but he [illegible] [illegible] in [illegible] [illegible] [illegible] and [illegible] [illegible] for a change in the [illegible] of the Baptist convention [illegible] year.

[illegible] his wife and with the approval of his family, Robert [illegible] the [illegible] of his [illegible] to the [illegible] [illegible] Rev. [illegible], who [illegible] [illegible] [illegible] Robert [illegible].

# JOEL'S STORY

The following story has a special meaning for me, primarily because it involves family. The incident that you are about to read occurred while I was working on this book. The story is about one of the nicest families you could ever want to meet: my brother-in-law, Hudy Bowlin, and his lovely wife, Patty. They have three wonderful children, Jeremy, Joel, and Letitia (Tish). I have been married to Hudy's sister for twenty-seven years, and you could say that Hudy and I have become pretty close—almost like brothers.

After Jeremy was born, doctors told Hudy and Patty that having more children might be fatal for her. If they wanted other children, they would have to adopt. After more than three years of trying to adopt a baby in the United States, Hudy and Patty decided to adopt from Honduras, where they found little Joel and Letitia. Both children were suffering from malnutrition, and it was obvious that their short time upon earth had not been an easy one. Hudy and Patty fell in love with them from the first moment they saw them.

When they returned to the United States, the Bowlin family numbered five. These three children could not have been raised in a more loving and caring home. Chief among the things they have been taught is love for God and the Bible.

Now, Hudy has always been a very religious person, and so is Patty. They are both strong people with a strong faith in God. On a warm night in June of 1997, they would find out just how strong their faith is. I honestly believe that a couple with a weaker faith could not have possibly survived the ordeal they had to face and, as of this writing, still face. Any doubts I may have had about the power of God and of prayer itself were answered for me by what has happened to this family.

I asked my brother-in-law if he would mind sharing this most remarkable story with the readers of this book. Though still tired and near exhaustion from his ordeal, he took the time to tell this story.

On the evening of June 24, 1997, my wife, Patty, and I received a call from Joey Allen, one of our son Joel's sparring partners at the Boys' and Girls' Club, where our son trains as an amateur boxer. I could hear urgency in Joey's voice as he informed me that our son had been injured and that he was being attended to at that very moment by a team of medics from the local Fire Department, which was located only a block from the club. Joey said the medics wanted to know which hospital they should take Joel to. Frantic, I told him that any hospital would be fine and to call me back as soon as he knew which one they had decided on. It seemed like hours before Joey called us back, but in reality it was less than ten minutes. Joey said they were taking our son to Memorial Hospital in Colorado Springs.

Patty and I, our elder son, Jeremy, and our daughter, Letitia, made the drive to the hospital Emergency Room in less than thirty minutes. Our minds were racing, and everyone in the car was praying. We hoped for a mild concussion, a fairly common injury in boxing.

We found that it was much worse than a simple concussion. Joel wasn't in the room. They had taken him to X ray his head. Soon the hospital staff returned him to the Emergency Room, and we could see that he was in a great deal of pain. They allowed us to talk with him. It hurt so much to see the pain he was in.

From the Emergency Room doctor we found out just how serious Joel's condition was. We were looking at a life or death situation. They had already called a neurosurgeon, and he was on his way to the hospital. They were going to have to operate immediately.

Seeing her brother in the Emergency Room, Tish became very upset. One of the nurses tried to calm her, but we thought her best at home until after the surgery. Our neighbors, Tony and Ann Buetti, gracious as always, came immediately to the hospital and took our daughter home with them.

The neurosurgeon briefed us on the situation. He showed us the X rays. There was bleeding inside the skull. The pressure from the bleeding was pressing against the right side of the brain. In fact, the brain was pushed to one side. The X ray clearly showed the brain was significantly displaced to the left. Without surgery, Joel would slip into a coma and never regain consciousness. They had to operate, or we would lose him.

The surgeon's name was Dr. Steven E. Murk. He was a very kind and gentle man. He apologized for being in a hurry. Of course, we were happy that he was in a hurry. While we signed the necessary papers, Dr. Murk ordered a room prepared for the surgery. At approximately 8:40 P.M., the nursing staff moved Joel into the surgery facility. At nine, the surgery began. At one point in the procedure, Dr. Murk called in an associate to help with the operation.

From the very beginning, God's children were praying for Joel and for us. After Joel was taken to the Emergency Room, Coach Copeland and Joel's teammates gathered there and prayed. As we were driving to the hospital, we were praying. When we first saw Joel lying in that hospital room and heard the doctor's words, we knew we were helpless to do anything except pray. That sounds strange, because calling upon our Heavenly Father is the most effective thing we can do, whether we are helpless or not.

During the early stages of the surgery, things were going well. A large part of Joel's skull was removed. The portion removed was approximately the size of a large horseshoe (directly above the right ear, to the rear of the head, through the top of the head, almost to the edge of the forehead).

Then things took a turn for the worse. During the surgery, Joel's brain began to swell. Dr. Murk later told us that had Joel been an adult, he would have stopped the procedure when the swelling became so severe. But, he said, he just couldn't quit. He knew if he had a fifteen-year-old boy, he would want the surgeon to do everything possible. And that was what he did. He removed the skull from the right temporal lobe. He did this to allow room for the swelling to expand. Unfortunately, the brain swelling continued until it had swelled beyond its normal brain cavity. As a result, Dr. Murk could not replace the portion of the skull that had been removed.

They had originally told us the operation would take three to four hours. After about three and one-half hours, one of the nurses came out of the operating room. She told us that things were not going well and that if we believed in calling on a higher power, this was the time to do it.

By the time Joel went into surgery, a number of people had arrived from our church, including the pastor, Pastor Landess.

On at least two occasions, we all gathered in a large circle and prayed for Joel. I found that I had mixed emotions. I knew that there was a very real possibility that Joel would not survive. Yet I felt an underlaying peace, the peace of God. I knew that no matter what happened that night, God was watching us and would help us through this ordeal.

About five hours into surgery, Coach Copeland came up to me and said, "I have been talking with the Lord, Hudy, and Joel is going to make it. He is going to be all right." I thanked him for his encouragement and told him that I was leaning on his faith. Later some of the boys came over and said, "Mr. Bowlin, Joel's going to be all right."

Finally, at about 2 A.M., the nurse from the operating room came to us again. The surgery was over. Dr. Murk wanted to talk to us. He had suggested that we bring our pastor with us. Those words sent a cold chill down my spine, but I knew I had to remain strong. Pastor Landess readily agreed to accompany us, and we felt that our son Jeremy should be with us as well.

Together we all followed the nurse to another waiting area. Dr. Murk entered shortly thereafter and sat down with us. He looked weary and concerned. We were desperately searching for something positive in that face, but it just wasn't there. Dr. Murk was as considerate as possible. However, after just a few minutes, we realized that Joel's chances of survival were not good.

There were a few moments of silence, then Dr. Murk, as gently as possible, began to explain what had transpired during the surgery. As he was talking, I suddenly felt myself becoming very hot, the room felt as if it were spinning, and everything was becoming fuzzy. I realized I was about to pass out. I wanted to tell Dr. Murk, but at the same time I didn't want to interrupt him. He was trying so hard to be kind, compassionate, and caring. Finally, I knew I was about to go out. My mind could not take the news we were hearing. It just wanted to shut down.

I interrupted Dr. Murk and said, "Excuse me, Doctor, but I think I'm about to pass out."

He immediately had me put my head between my legs. I sat like that for a few minutes. Dr. Murk put his arm around my shoulders and continued talking while watching me closely. Patty began to rub my back. After several minutes, I began to feel more alert.

The doctor then led us to the Trauma Intensive Care Unit (TICU), to which they had moved Joel following the operation. As we walked down the hallway, I couldn't help but think, "At least he's not taking us to the morgue. There is still hope."

Dr. Murk had told us that it would be several hours before Joel regained consciousness. Patty and I spent some time alone with Joel. You cannot truly express the feelings that race through your mind and body when you stand silently over your child and stare down at him. Something grips your very soul and tears at your heart. Every fiber in you wants to do something—anything—to stop that child's pain. It is at that very moment that you realize just how helpless you really are.

Leaving Patty with Joel, I went to the waiting room to update our friends and Joel's teammates on his condition. I thanked them for their prayers and requested that they continue to pray for our son. Coach Copeland and a number of Joel's friends remained in the waiting area for the rest of the night.

Sometime before 6 A.M., Joel began to come around. He immediately got sick, vomiting what little fluids there were left in his stomach.

At seven, Ann Buetti called and told us that Tish was having a difficult time dealing with all of this. She had stayed awake until two and then woken up before six. Worry and exhaustion were taking their toll. My wife and I agreed that it would be best to take Tish back to our home.

As I began the thirty-minute drive to the Buettis' home, the events of the night replayed themselves in my mind and a wave of emotion suddenly swept over me. I began to cry like a baby. I cried all the way to the Buettis. I kept thinking of the first time I had ever seen Joel. We were in Honduras, going through the adoption process for Joel and Tish. Joel was only twenty-seven months old. He cried and cried the entire time I held him. I kept thinking of that little boy who had cried in my arms for two hours straight. Then I saw that same boy so helplessly lying in that hospital bed with all those tubes running in and out of him. I kept saying, "Lord, if it is your will to take Joel home with you, please give me the strength to withstand the pain."

My heart ached so bad for that little boy that I felt I could not endure the pain. But even then I continued to feel a peace, knowing that God was in control and that his will is always best. I understood now how painful true faith can be. We have always known that our children are a gift from the Lord and that he has the right to take them home anytime he chooses. But our children are so dear to us. I found myself wondering if God hurt this bad when he allowed his Son to die on the cross for our sins. Then I realized he must have hurt worse, because the Father and Son had been together in perfect love for all eternity. I wondered how God the Father could have given up his only Son to such torture and cruelty. I am thankful that God is God and that I am not God. I know now that I could not possibly have done what our Heavenly Father did.

By the time I arrived at the Buettis, I couldn't say more than two words without crying. I quickly took Tish home, and she immediately fell into her bed, fast asleep. I slumped into a chair and rested a few hours, then took our daughter to our pastor's home where his wife had so graciously offered to take care of her for us. I then returned to the hospital.

Joel had regained consciousness.

At about ten that night, the surgeon came by to see how Joel was doing. I was in the waiting room at the time, making a phone call. A nurse hurried up to me and told me that the doctor wanted to see me. As I entered TICU through the big double doors, I saw the surgeon standing just outside Joel's unit.

He said, "There must have been a lot of praying going on last night. To be honest, I never expected Joel to regain consciousness." He paused for a moment and, looking at Joel, continued, "Over the years, I have noticed things happening that are beyond my control. This is one of those things."

We knew that God had responded to the many prayers of his children. God had chosen to spare Joel's life. We did not know why, but we thanked him over and over.

During this ordeal, hundreds of prayers were going up to our Heavenly Father for Joel. Coach Copeland's wife called her husband's mother in Detroit. She in turn contacted friends and her church. They all started praying for Joel. I called my sister in Ada, Oklahoma. She asked her church to pray. Phyllis Didlo, who is a friend of the family and lives in Black Forest, Colorado, asked her church to pray for Joel.

Over the next two weeks, we met so many people who said their church was praying for Joel. Of course, many people in our own church (Norwood Bible Church) were praying for our son.

Looking back now, I can see that our Heavenly Father was answering prayer from the very beginning. The medics were only one block away and got to Joel within minutes of the 911 call. They were able to stabilize him quickly and get him to the hospital within a short period of time. Dr. Murk was in the general area and got to the hospital in minutes. He was the surgeon on call, a doctor who not only is compassionate, but refused to give up when things went bad during the operation.

Members of our church came to the hospital quickly and joined Joel's friends, his coach, and our family in prayer for him. These dear people spent the night in prayer in support of us. We are truly thankful for the company of these godly people and for their encouragement. We felt God's strength in our lives in response to these prayers. I have never considered myself a strong person. Now I know all the more how true that is. I knew that the peace I was experiencing was not from me, but from the one true Father.

The seven days after Joel's surgery proved to be the most difficult of my life. Yet during that time, I experienced more of God's strength than at any other time in my life. Patty and I were getting only about three or four hours sleep a night, and many of those were often interrupted.

The doctors, nurses, and staff were amazed by how well Joel was doing so soon after surgery. Within days, he was alert and could actually write messages to us with a pad and pen, even though he was still hooked up to

IVs and had respirator tubes still in his lungs. These were wonderful developments, but also we saw that he was easily agitated. We sought to comfort him, but there was little we could do.

After a few days, the respirator tubes were removed from Joel's lungs. He was now breathing on his own.

Yes, we were excited and relieved. However, after a few days in the TICU, Joel became very upset at night. He would attempt to climb out of his bed. Although he could not move his left arm and left leg, he could still get out of bed. Joel was a very strong boy. He played football and worked out often to stay in shape. At night when he was agitated, he would throw his right leg over the bed rail, then he would grab the bed rail with his right hand, next he would flex his right arm and leg, and over he would go. That is, until we caught him in midair. We learned very quickly to keep an eye on that right leg. When it began to go over the bed rail, we would grab him. When we pulled him back onto the bed, he would become upset and try to get away from us. We knew we had to restrain him, because if his head hit the floor, the impact to his unprotected brain area could easily be fatal.

Frequently, it would take three or four of us to restrain him while a nurse gave him a shot. The sedative would work for an hour to an hour and a half, then this would begin all over again. One night, Joel was so wild that the nurse's aide put a restraining jacket on him and strapped him to the bed. It took almost ten minutes to get it on him and tie him down. When he realized that he was strapped down, he gave one sharp twist with his body and broke one of the restraining straps. Off came what was left of the jacket.

One nurse suggested that they place a heavier restraining jacket on him, but the head nurse rejected that idea. She thought the risk of him hurting himself trying to escape the restraints would be the greater. Keep in mind that Joel still had a horseshoe-sized piece of his skull missing.

This type of activity went on for four or five nights. After each of these episodes, I found myself totally drained. It would take me about an hour to relax after Joel was sedated. I would then try to doze off for a few minutes, but just as I began to nod off, Joel would awake from the sedative and try for the rail again.

We quickly learned the warning signs. First we would hear a groan. When we heard that, we knew we had only seconds to react before he began his attempt. I would jump to his bedside and grab a leg or arm, whichever I could reach first. Then the wrestling match would begin again. There were always two of us in the room, myself and a sitter. We would immediately press the nurses' call button. Two or three nurses and aides would immediately come to the room. Three or four of us would restrain him. One person would attempt to calm him.

The head nurse, Dee, was especially good at talking to him and helping him to calm down. However, there were nights when even her calming words had no effect. After four straight nights of this, no matter how tired I was, I did not want to fall asleep, because I knew I would be awakened at any second and find myself in another struggle with Joel. What made it even worse was the fact that when I went home during the day, I had so much adrenaline pumping through me that it took me hours to calm down.

At times, I wondered if I could take another night. There were moments when I was overcome by waves of despair. When those moments came, I had to fall on my knees before the Heavenly Father and cry out for help. And each time he answered my prayer. He would help me cope with the moment at hand.

On the night of July 13, when Patty was sitting with Joel, our son was in a mood to talk. He told his mother that something had happened to him during surgery. He told her that he had seen Jesus playing with a group of children on the seashore. Then Jesus came over to him, put his arm around him, and said, "Your suffering is for me."

When Patty told me this, I felt tears rushing to my eyes. She couldn't keep from crying, herself.

Joel also told his mother of another experience he had had on a previous night. A sitter by the name of Tina was with him. He had become very fond of Tina. On that particular night, Joel had a severe headache. He was in a lot of pain.

He asked Tina, "Who is that?"

Tina said, "Where?"

Joel pointed to one of the walls of the room and said, "Over there."

Tina told him there was no one else in the room.

Joel later recalled that he had seen a man standing there, very average-looking but with the most compassionate eyes. The man had then walked over to Joel's bedside and gently brushed the palm of his hand across the top of Joel's head. Joel said that at that instant the pain in his head went away and he felt a great peace in his heart.

After the miracles that had occurred since the beginning of this ordeal, we had no trouble believing that one of God's angels had touched our son Joel.

Joel Bowlin spent six days in the TICU. He was then moved to the seventh floor, where head-trauma patients are cared for. After twelve days there, this remarkable young man was moved to the Rehabilitation Hospital of Colorado Springs.

Amazingly, Joel has begun his rehabilitation and has regained some feeling in his left arm and leg. Although there is still a long road ahead for Joel and his family, there is no doubt in my mind that they will overcome all obstacles, for their belief in God and the power of their faith will keep them strong.

I ask that all readers remember them in their prayers.

## THE GRADUATE

On a cold November night in 1995, Carolyn Walker and two girlfriends were on their way home from church services. Everyone was in a joyous holiday mood. School was out for the holidays and Thanksgiving was only a few days away. For Carolyn, it was an extra-special time. Her boyfriend and childhood sweetheart, Brian, was coming home for the first time since beginning his freshman year at the University of Alabama. It had been two long, lonely months since they had seen each other, and Carolyn could hardly contain herself. The couple had agreed that they would wait until Brian was at least a senior at Alabama before they set a wedding date, much to the relief of both sets of parents. But when one is in love, waiting can be a torturous ordeal—an ordeal that serves to make the special times together all the more special. Like Thanksgiving.

Carolyn Walker was a typical young woman of seventeen. She came from an upper-middle-class family and had been raised in an atmosphere in which love, manners, and religion were taught from an early age. Trim and attractive, Carolyn had always been an active participant in school events from the glee club and cheerleading to the debating team. She was well liked by all who knew her and had a personality that won over everyone she met. It was no wonder that Brian constantly talked about her at college. She was a girl every young man would be happy to know.

On this night, a light snow had fallen, adding to the seven inches that had already fallen the day before. The fresh snow gave everything the appearance of a winter wonderland, a scene straight out of a Norman Rockwell painting. But often things of beauty can also be hazardous, as the three young ladies were about to discover.

Carolyn was laughing about something her friend, Tina Savage, had just said. She had only taken her eyes off the road for a moment to glance at Tina, but that one moment was all it took. Carolyn never saw the patch of ice that had formed just beyond the curve in the road. Suddenly, she had no control of her car. It careened across the highway. Slamming into a section of guardrail, the car veered back across the highway and off the road at an angle, then flipped on its side and rolled over four times before coming to rest against a stand of trees some thirty yards down the embankment.

Where only seconds before there had been the sounds of breaking glass and crunching metal mixed with the screams of three terrified girls, there was now only silence. The only sign that anything had happened was a section of guardrail missing at the top of the embankment and a strange, almost eerie light from the car's headlights that cast its glare through the treetops.

It was this strange light that first drew the attention of young Ricky Strictland as he came around the same curve. Slowing down, he pulled off the side of the road for a better look. Stepping out of his car, he immediately noticed the missing section of guardrail a few yards ahead of where he had parked. Following the beam of light into the trees, he could make out the shape of a car.

"Oh, my God!" he cried, and he grabbed for his cell phone. Dialing 911, he reported the location of the accident and asked for help. The operator began asking him questions that he had no answers to. "Just send help!" he yelled into the phone. "From the condition of that car, someone's hurt, I'm sure. Just get somebody out here."

Shoving the phone into his pocket, Ricky made his way down the slippery embankment. The first person he found was Tina. She had been thrown from the car on the second or third roll, and it was clear that she was dead. The car had rolled over her. Farther down, he could smell the overpowering odor of gasoline. The car wasn't smoking, but that didn't mean anything. It could still explode at any minute. His prime concern was getting whoever was left in the car out and as far away as possible.

The driver's side of the car was his only point of entrance. The passenger side was jammed solid against the side of a huge tree. Peering through the shattered glass on the driver's side, Ricky could see that there were two girls still in the car. Both were bloody and unconscious. Struggling with the bent door, he finally managed to get it open. Carolyn was still strapped in her seat belt. Undoing the belt, Ricky started to move her, then stopped. There was something about the way her neck was leaning to one side that didn't seem right.

"Her neck's broken," he whispered to himself.

Using a piece of broken glass, he made a cut across the seat. Pulling the foam padding from the seat, he placed it gently around Carolyn's neck, then cut a piece of the seat belt and carefully wrapped it around the foam until he had formed a thick collar. Satisfied that it was the best he could do to limit her neck movement, Ricky carefully eased his hands under her legs and back and removed her from the car.

Carrying her a good thirty feet from the car, he placed her on the snow-covered ground and returned for the other girl.

Sally Compton, Carolyn's other girlfriend, was in bad shape. She had multiple face and head cuts and had lost a lot of blood. As Ricky was removing her from the car, he found that she also had a compound fracture of the right leg just below the knee. It was a frightful injury, and he was grateful that she was unconscious. He had just placed Sally on the ground next to Carolyn and got out his cell phone to place another call to 911 when he heard the sirens approaching and could see the flashing lights among the treetops above. Lights suddenly began to appear along the top of the embankment, first one, two, then three, four, until soon there seemed to be an army at the top of the hill.

"Down here!" he yelled, "Hurry! They're hurt bad."

Eight hours after the fateful crash, Carolyn Walker and Sally Compton lay unconscious in separate rooms at Saint Francis Hospital, distraught parents at their bedsides. Downstairs, another family grieved. For Tina's family, there was no hospital room to visit; they had been taken to the morgue.

In the morning, the doctors called the families together and briefed them on their children's injuries. Although Sally had appeared to be worse injured at the crash site because of the amount of blood on her, other than the compound fracture and cuts she had received from flying glass, which required more than one hundred stitches she was not badly injured.

For Carolyn, the diagnosis was not as promising. Ricky had been right. Carolyn's neck was broken. She had also received injuries to her ribs, spleen, and a kidney. A team of doctors had worked on her for six hours in the operating room in a gallant effort to stop internal bleeding and protect the few uninjured fibers of her spinal column. They all agreed that it was a miracle that Carolyn Walker was still alive. Of all her injuries, the broken neck was the worst. It had left her paralyzed from the neck down, and they had little hope that she would ever recover.

The following day, Brian arrived at the hospital. Carolyn was still unconscious, but he remained at her bedside for two days, refusing to leave her. As word of the accident spread, friends, classmates, and teachers came by or sent cards and flowers until the room was filled with them. Carolyn awoke from her coma, but when she learned of her condition, she sank quickly into a deep depression out of which no one, not even Brian, could bring her. There was very little hope for recovery and she knew it. Days turned into weeks, and there seemed to be little progress.

A specialist in spinal column injuries was brought in. Three months and two operations later, doctors could see no change in Carolyn's condition. Her other injuries had been taken care of, and they were healing nicely, but that meant little to the young woman who could not move. The nurses often would come into her room at night and find her pillow wet from the tears that had run down her lovely face. They would leave the room with tears in their eyes as well.

Five months after the accident, Brian came for a visit. He had two other young men with him from the University of Alabama. They were members of Brian's Bible study group, which he attended two nights a week. Carolyn's parents happened to be there that day when the boys came in. They couldn't help but notice that Brian seemed unusually upbeat and almost joyous. This was indeed quite a change from the despondent young man of only a few weeks before.

Moving to Carolyn's side, Brian took her hand in his and, kissing her gently on the forehead, smiled and whispered, "It's going to be all right, Carolyn. You're going to walk again. We're going to organize a prayer circle that will span the country, and God in his mercy is going to heal you. I promise."

Carolyn's mother was horrified. Grabbing Brian by the arm, she pulled him aside and in an angry tone scolded him for making such promises to her poor, helpless daughter. It wasn't only cruel, but heartless as well. How could he make such a promise? And what kind of Bible study course had he been taking anyway? Didn't he think they had already prayed for a miracle? Brian calmed her, then informed her that his friends, Mike and Paul, were members of the new Charismatic Church, which believed in modern-day miracles through the power of God and prayer. If anyone could help Carolyn now, it was God and only God, but they would have to ask for that help.

Carolyn's father stepped to his wife's side and placed his arm around Brian. "Mother, let the boys do what they feel is right. We've tried everything else."

That afternoon, Brian, Mike, and Paul stood at the sides and foot of Carolyn's bed and prayed for two hours, placing their hands on her feet, legs, shoulders, and hands as they prayed. At three in the afternoon, they placed a call to their church group at the University. By five, calls and messages had been sent out on the Internet to all other members across the country. At nine that night, they would hold a special service for the healing of Carolyn Walker. By eight, the Walkers, the preacher from their church, and a number of church members were waiting in Carolyn's room and in the hallways for the praying hour to arrive. As the hour drew near, they were joined by a host of nurses from each floor of the hospital and two of the doctors who had operated on Carolyn since the accident.

At nine, with Brian at her bedside holding her hand, the prayer service began. With tears of both joy and hope flowing down her cheeks, Carolyn Walker closed her eyes and prayed harder than she had ever prayed in her life. Suddenly, halfway through the service, her eyes opened wide, and she smiled the biggest smile of her life.

Brian leaned over her. "What is it, Carolyn? What's happened?"

"I heard him," she whispered. "He spoke to me, Brian. I know he did. I felt a warm, almost burning sensation down my back. Oh, Brian, I believe God just touched me."

The room had gone absolutely silent. Brian asked, "What did he say, Carolyn? Tell us."

Choking back the tears, she struggled to get the words out. "He said I will be all right. I will walk again."

A great feeling of joy and thanksgiving spread over the room and into the hallway and throughout the hospital as word of what had happened was relayed to each floor and each ward. At that very moment, there was a feeling that God himself was among them all. The service continued, now to give thanks to God for his intervention. Of course, Carolyn still could not move, but that didn't matter. She would. God had said so.

The next morning, Dr. Thomas Selmon, Carolyn's specialist, came in to see her. She was smiling for the first time since he had met her. "Well, I hear we had a little excitement in here last night. Seems you had a very important visitor. Is that right?"

Her smile broadened. "That's right, Dr. Selmon. A real VIP, you might say."

Not wanting to shatter the young woman's dream, Dr. Selmon wasn't sure how to deal with this situation. He'd heard the story about the service first thing that morning from practically everyone he spoke to. But now what? Dr. Selmon had grown very fond of this young woman, who had shown so much promise in her life. Oh, if only she were to walk again, he thought to himself. But what if nothing happened? Frustrated expectations could send her into a state of depression from which she might never return. Then what would they do?

From the tray of instruments that sat beside the bed, the doctor picked up the small rubber hammer that he had used to test Carolyn's reflexes over the last four months. Uncovering her feet, he held the rubber end of the hammer in the palm of his hand and, placing the chrome end at the heel of her right foot, he brought it slowly up the arch of her foot. Just as he feared, nothing happened. He moved to the left foot and did the same thing. Again there was no reaction. Across the room, Brian, Mike, Paul, and the Walkers stood silently, observing the procedure. A small tear made its way down Mrs. Walker's face. Brian took her hand in his and squeezed it tight. Dr. Selmon looked up at Carolyn; she was still smiling.

"Would you do that again, please?" she asked.

The doctor quickly ran the cold steel up both feet again. "Carolyn, did you feel that?" he asked excitedly. "Tell me you felt something—anything!"

Carolyn began to cry. "I do feel something—I do! Oh, God, thank you! Thank you!"

By that afternoon, the slight feeling Carolyn Walker had felt in the soles of her feet in the morning was so much stronger that when the doctor ran the instrument up the sole, the foot would arch, showing signs of sensitivity. Within a few days, she began to have tingling sensations in the tips of her fingers and by week's end could form both hands into fists and wiggle her toes.

Dr. Selmon was astounded by the rapid rate at which all these functions began to reappear. He called in a number of colleagues to observe what was happening to Carolyn and confirm that there were no known medical reasons to explain any of it.

The following week, Carolyn continued to improve at a rapid rate and was soon sitting up and feeding herself. To look at her, no one would have guessed why she was in the hospital. When Dr. Selmon solicited his colleagues for answers, they had none. Only one doctor made an effort to explain the remarkable turn of events. It was possible, he said, that they had misdiagnosed the injury; perhaps the nerves had only been traumatized and with time had begun to return to normal.

Perhaps he was right. What do you think?

Carolyn fully recovered from her ordeal and finished high school, graduating at the top of her class. She and Brian were married in January 1997. Today Brian and Carolyn are students at the University of Alabama. In October 1997 their first child was born—a six-pound, four-ounce bouncing baby girl named Hope. The couple expect to graduate in 2001. They are still active in the church and Bible group. To this day Carolyn remains convinced of the power of prayer and the role it played in her life.

## JUDY'S STORY

For Judy Renfro, June 15, 1990 will always remain one of the darkest days of her life. On that day, the thirty-seven-year-old single mother of three was told that she had inoperable cancer. Her doctor showed her the X rays from her previous exam and pointed out not one but two spots on the film that revealed a malignant cancer. The first was located on the lower left side of her neck, the second, midway down her spine.

Hearing the news, she stared blankly at the X rays, as if her mind did not—would not—accept what the doctor had just told her. Dr. Tanner gave Judy a few minutes to accept his diagnosis then told her that they would have to begin her cobalt treatments as soon as possible. He would like to start on the neck area first, then move to the spine. She would have to come in every other day for the treatments. Would that be a problem for her?

Judy almost broke down in tears. A problem? Yes, it would be a problem, just as having to divorce a husband of fifteen years because he had become a violent alcoholic had been a problem. Just as having to raise three children by herself had been a problem, and having to work two jobs for the first year after the divorce because that same husband had run them into debt and ruined her credit had been a problem. Oh, yes, it would be a problem, but like every other problem, she had no choice but to accept it and deal with it as best she could.

On the drive home, Judy cried and kept asking herself why this had happened just when everything was finally coming together. She had a great new job, a new car, and a credit rating that was finally acceptable to every credit card company in the country. Why, after struggling so hard for so long to make things right, why had God let this happen to her? He knew what she had gone through these last five years. Why was she now being punished?

There were so many things that had to be attended too. School was out for the summer. She'd have to contact her sister to watch the kids. Then there was her job. She'd have to make arrangements to be off a few hours every other day for the treatments. She wasn't sure how her employer would take that. Then there were the financial aspects to consider. Treatment was not going to be cheap, but how much would it be? How much would her insurance cover? And finally, just how sick would she eventually become from both the cancer and the cobalt treatments? So many things to think about—to do—to worry about. By the time she pulled the car into her driveway, Judy Renfro was on the verge of a mental breakdown, feeling lower than she had at any time in her life.

That night, she gathered her children, Matt (fourteen), Karen (twelve), and Brian (ten), around the kitchen table. As they all held hands, Judy explained to them what the doctor had told her and what was going to be happening over the next few weeks and perhaps longer. Judy had always found it best to be straightforward with her children. After all, anything that happened to one affected them all. At first they cried, which was to be expected, the fear of losing their mother plain in their young eyes. But Judy managed to calm them as usual and convince them that her treatments would more than likely take care of the cancer and that she would be fine. It would just be a little difficult around the house for a while, and she was going to need their help to keep things running smoothly for the next few weeks. They compiled a list of tasks each child was to be responsible for, and by the time they went to bed, the children were still worried but confident that their mother would overcome this problem, as she had so many others.

Judy then called her sister Carol and gave her the news. Carol arrived at Judy's within the hour. They both hugged and cried for a while, then talked about what had to be done if and when Judy's health should begin to fail, as well as, the unthinkable, if she should die. Carol rejected this last thought, but Judy finally made her realize that they had to face reality and prepare for the worst.

Judy's next call was to her mother. Her father had died of cancer only two years earlier, and this was a call she flinched from making, but it too had to be done. Judy's mother lived in California. Her reaction was the same as Carol's. First disbelief, then tears, and finally acceptance. Her mother would be flying to Oklahoma on the first flight out the following morning.

By the time Judy went to bed that night, she was a total wreck. Her emotions ran the gamut; first tears and sadness, then bitterness, which quickly turned to shameful self-pity, then back to tears again, until finally, from sheer exhaustion, Judy Renfro fell asleep.

Judy's employer was most sympathetic to her situation and assured her that her job was secure and that the company's insurance would cover nearly all of her medical expenses. That alone gave Judy her first sense of relief since her ordeal had begun. Then too, having her mother home with her made her realize that she wasn't facing this alone.

Over the next few weeks, Judy underwent eleven cobalt treatments. She began to experience a constant sore throat, and certain muscles began to collapse. She seemed tired all the time and would become irritable and testy with those around her, but they all understood. There was always the constant battle with self-pity—a feeling that she was being punished without knowing why.

One night, as Judy and her mother sat at the table, her mother asked, "Dear, have you asked God to help with this?" Judy appeared uncomfortable with the question at first, then told her mother that she had thought of praying at the beginning, but then it seemed praying would be a waste of time. If God was there to help her, he wouldn't have let this happen to begin with.

Judy's mother was taken aback by her daughter's reply, but was certain that answer came more from bitterness than belief. Her mother left the room for a moment then returned with a faded, well-worn edition of the King James Bible.

Placing the book on the table, she said, "Darling, the doctors and modern medicine can only do so much. In the end, it is God that will make the difference." She then kissed

Judy on the forehead and went to bed, leaving her daughter to ponder her words.

Judy sat quietly staring at the large book in front of her then ran her hand over the cover of the family heirloom. She found it hard to convince herself that what the brightest doctors and most advanced medical technology could not accomplish this book could. Small pieces of paper protruded from the end of the Bible, identifying certain passages and verses her mother had marked for her. But she was too tired to read now, she thought, she'd do it tomorrow. Tidying up the kitchen, she started to turn out the light, but her eyes came to rest on the Bible once more. In that moment, she felt a sudden tingling surge through her body. It startled her at first but at the same time seemed to spread a sense of calm and well-being throughout her body that she had not known for weeks.

Before she realized it, Judy was at the table again and had opened the Bible to the first marker placed by her mother. With each verse and story she read, she began to feel a resurgence of strength and confidence that this was a battle that she could win with God's help. By morning, Judy's faith had grown by leaps and bounds, and nothing in the world seemed impossible. Judy was bright-eyed and bubbling with excitement when her mother came into the kitchen that morning. Hugging her mother with tears in her eyes, she said, "Mother, you were so right! Nothing is impossible with God."

That morning marked a change in Judy Renfro's life that has lasted to this day. It was a sudden transformation, which was noticed immediately by the doctors, her coworkers, and her family. Prayer sessions became a nightly ritual around the Renfro kitchen table and included not only family, but the pastor and members of the congregation of the local church that Judy had attended before her divorce. They all prayed specifically that God would heal her.

Then one night, as Judy lay in bed, silently giving praise to God for uplifting her spirit, she felt a strange sensation spreading over her body. It was a warm but pleasing feeling that washed from the bottom of her feet to the top of her head and back again. Two months ago, this would have scared her to death, but there was no fear that night. Judy knew in her heart that God had answered her prayers and the many prayers of her family, friends, and neighbors. God had healed her. She was certain of that.

The news spread quickly among the prayer group, and everyone waited with bated breath for the end of the week, when Judy would enter the hospital for another series of tests. The tests were supposed to locate the malignancies and evaluate which of the two was spreading the faster. But Judy, her mother, and many in the prayer group knew in their hearts that the doctor's tests would show that Judy had been healed.

On Friday morning, Judy was checked into the hospital, and the tests began. After a grueling six hours, Judy was resting in her room when the radiologist, accompanied by her doctor, came to give her the results.

There was nothing there. Nothing. Not one sign that Judy had ever had cancer could be found. Nor was there the slightest sign that this woman had been subjected to cobalt treatments.

Her doctor was at a loss for an explanation, but to be certain, he wanted her to remain overnight and submit to the same battery of tests again the following day. With a smile, in a tired but joyous voice, Judy agreed and assured both men that the results would be the same.

The following afternoon, Judy Renfro and her mother left the hospital arm in arm and giving thanks to God all the way home, where a sister and three very excited children were waiting.

Eight years later, Judy has never again shown any signs of cancer. She has received two promotions. One of her sons has graduated from the University of Oklahoma, her daughter will do the same next year, and her younger son will enter Oklahoma State University the year after.

For Judy Renfro, prayer and God's love changed her life. She has not missed a Sunday service in eight years. And I, for one, don't think she ever will.

## THE MYSTERIOUS REVEREND

One of the most amazing stories I have come across is a little-known incident that occurred in the Texas town of Advil.

Advil has just over nine hundred residents. Like all Texans, they possess that special quality that makes Texas such a great state: You're greeted with a warm, friendly smile, a loud "Howdy, partner!" and a firm handshake. Advil is also a strongly religious community that supports its church and school activities with an enthusiasm that could easily serve as a perfect example for the rest of the country.

But on one particular warm summer day in mid-June of 1995, the residents of Advil, Texas, lost their normal enthusiasm, and their spirits were low. In such a small community, everyone knew practically everyone else. Such was the case with Paul and Mary Thorton. The couple had been born and raised in Advil. Their children had grown up and attended school there as well. Now grown and married, the kids were gone, leaving Paul and Mary with a lifetime of wonderful memories and plenty of time to become heavily involved in the activities of their town and church.

Paul served as a member of the city council, a member of the church board of directors, and a church activities organizer. Mary headed the numerous charitable organizations that the church had been involved with over the years. Needless to say, the couple, who were in their midsixties, were well known to the entire community and dearly loved.

It was while working on a food drive in early May of 1995 that Mary Thorton first noticed the sharp pain that sent a stinging sensation shooting down her left arm. Her fingers began to tingle, then seemed to go numb for a moment. Shocked by the sudden, unexpected pain, Mary clutched her arm and leaned back against the wall.

It was a movement that did not go unnoticed by Alice Calder, a close friend. Walking over to Mary, she asked, "Mary, are you all right? What is it?"

In an attempt to fool herself as well as her old friend, Mary forced a smile and calmly replied, "Oh, it's nothing, Alice. I must have hit my elbow against the door. Stings like the dickins, but really, it's nothing."

Alice did not seemed convinced, but wasn't going to push the matter. It was clear to her that Mary did not want to discuss it any further.

Later, driving home, Mary kept flexing the fingers of her left hand. The numbness was just about gone, along with the burning pain in her arm. "What in the world could have caused that terrible pain?" she asked herself as she turned her car onto the road home. Of course, she had an idea, but she didn't want to think about that. Her heart was as strong as ever. She had never smoked, she ate all the right foods, exercised, and had never in her life had any type of problem with her breathing. Yet the incident had all the characteristics of a warning sign of a possible stroke.

By the time Mary had pulled the car into her garage, she had convinced herself that the pain was nothing more than severe indigestion from the spicy chili they had had for lunch. She saw no reason to worry Paul about such a minor thing. After all, it had only lasted for a fleeting second or two and had not recurred in five hours. No—it must have been the chili.

Weeks passed, and soon Mary forgot the incident. Forgot it, that is, until the day of the annual Advil founder's day picnic, a day-long event that was the highlight of Advil's summer celebrations. Everyone gathered at the community park located in the center of the town square. There was music, dancing, games, and quantities of food. It seemed as though everyone in town was there that day.

Paul was by the horseshoe pits, keeping score and serving as official judge of the event. Mary, Alice, and the rest of the ladies' club were busy judging and awarding ribbons for the numerous craft exhibits that were located throughout the park. By noon, the heat in west Texas had passed ninety-eight degrees and was still climbing.

Mary was holding a hand-molded clay pot in her hands, admiring the beautiful painted design, when her attack struck. The pot dropped to the ground, shattering into a hundred pieces. Mary's face suddenly turned ashen-gray. She grabbed at her chest. Her mouth opened, but no sound came out. Gasping for breath, she felt herself waver as if the earth were rocking under her feet. A few seconds later, she dropped to the ground, unconscious.

Alice was the first to scream for help. Two of the men standing nearby rushed to the horseshoe pit to get Paul. Slowly, as word spread, all activity in the park came to a halt as concerned friends and neighbors gathered around Mary. Richard W. Pierce, the local doctor, was at Mary's side when Paul made his way through the crowd. Kneeling next to his wife and sweetheart of nearly fifty years and holding her hand, Paul asked, "What is it, Doctor? What's happened to my sweet Mary?"

Dr. Pierce felt a weak pulse and observed the twisted left hand and the deformed facial muscles on the right side of Mary's face. "A stroke, Paul. I believe Mary has had a very severe stroke." Tears welled up in Paul's eyes, and a soft muttering of whispers spread through the crowd gathered around them.

Within minutes, an ambulance arrived, and Mary was taken to Dr. Pierce's clinic. Because it is a small community, Advil did not have a hospital. For the moment, the clinic was the best they could do until the doctor could make arrangements to have Mary transported to the hospital in Amarillo.

To Paul, the trip to the clinic seemed to take forever. A long procession of vehicles followed the ambulance. Once there, Dr. Pierce had Mary rushed straight to X ray.

One of the many people in the room with Paul was the Reverend Charles Graham, pastor of Mary and Paul's church. Clutching Paul's hand tightly in his own, the reverend raised their hands in the air and addressed the crowd that had gathered in the room and overflowed into the hallway.

"My dear friends, let us pray for our sister Mary. Pray as you've never prayed before."

Reverend Graham began his prayer. The townspeople held hands, bowed their heads, and prayed silently along with him. Just as the prayer ended, the doctor came into the room. The grim look on his face almost sent Paul to his knees. It was bad news, and Paul knew it. "What is it, Richard?"

Dr. Pierce slowly shook his head. "I'm afraid I was right, Paul. Mary has had a severe stroke. She has sustained substantial damage."

Paul's voice trembled as he asked, "She's not going to . . . die . . . is she, Doctor? Please, God. Not that. Tell me I'm not going to lose her, Doctor. Please."

A hush fell over the people gathered at the clinic. Dr. Pierce could not make himself look his old friend in the eye. He knew Paul would see the truth if he did. Looking away, he answered, "I can't say, Paul. We'll just have to wait and see. But I won't lie to you. It's not good. Not good at all."

As Dr. Pierce left the room, he could hear the soft, almost silent sobs of many of Mary Thorton's friends. He was going to keep her at the clinic for a few hours in the hope that her condition would stabilize, then they would transport her to Amarillo. Until then, the doctor wanted the room cleared of everyone but Paul and Reverend Graham. The people were welcome to remain at the clinic to pray, just not in Mary's room. Some people left the hallway for the small chapel located across the street from the clinic. Others gathered in a circle in the parking lot to continue their prayer vigil for Mary Thorton.

Paul and Reverend Graham stood silently in a corner of the room as nurses brought in more heart monitoring equipment and began attaching the wires and tabs to Mary's body. Paul had never felt so totally helpless in his life. There lay the woman he had idolized and loved for fifty years, and now, when she needed him most, he could do nothing but stand by and watch as others tended to her. For a moment he thought of calling the kids, but he couldn't make himself do it. That would be the same as saying it was over, that there was no hope. Yet Paul still felt that surely God in all his mercy would look down upon this wonderful woman, who had given so unselfishly of herself her entire life, and answer the prayers of the people of Advil, Texas, who called upon him to spare this woman's life.

The minutes stretched into hours, and soon it was night, but still no one left the parking lot or chapel. The prayer vigil for Mary continued as strong as ever. The doctor came in a few times to check on her, and each time his expression held less hope than the time before. Finally, at nine o'clock, the doctor came in, checked Mary's pulse and her eyes, then listened to her heart. Sadly he turned to Paul and informed him that if he needed to call any other members of the family, he should do it now.

The words struck Paul like a sledgehammer to the heart. He suddenly felt dizzy, and his knees almost buckled. He was going to lose her—he realized that now. Clutching Reverend Graham's shoulders, he pleaded with the man of God to do something.

"Make God listen," he pleaded. "Please God, don't take her from us, please!" The strain was more than Paul could stand.

He broke down and began to weep like a small child. Reverend Graham held him in a firm but gentle grasp, crying right along with him.

At this point, all seemed lost. Dr. Pierce had even called the hospital in Amarillo and informed it that the expected transfer to that facility would not be necessary. Judging from his patient's vital signs, Mary Thorton would pass away before midnight.

At about the same time as Dr. Pierce was completing his call to Amarillo, a late-model black Chevy van pulled into the clinic parking lot. The van appeared to be brand-new. Slowly the crowd in the parking lot began to part, allowing it to proceed to the front door of the clinic. It had heavily tinted windows, so no one could see the driver or tell how many people were inside the vehicle. One thing was certain, this van was not from around Advil; and it was not a vehicle that the locals would easily forget. Its gloss was almost blinding. Equally bright were the solid chrome wheels that held the tires.

John Tanner, a local rancher, remembers looking for a license plate to see where the van was from, but there were no plates on the vehicle anywhere. Others also remember not seeing a license plate.

The van sat at the curb for a few minutes after the engine stopped. Then the driver's door opened, and a tall, lanky man in his early thirties emerged. He was dressed all in black. The crowd pressed forward to get a better look at the stranger who had entered their town at this time of crisis. The one thing each person would remember about this man was his eyes. They were deep-set and as coal-black as the van he was driving. His hair was long, flowing over the back of his collar. He glanced around for a moment at the crowd, then seemed to nod, as if in approval, but at no time did his stern expression ever show any type of emotion or reaction. Many would later say it was a serious expression. That was the only way to explain it.

The man never spoke a word. The crowd parted before him as he made his way to the double glass doors and walked inside, all the time ignoring the murmurs that followed him. Who was this man? Had anyone ever seen the van before? Where was he from? One elderly lady in the crowd was clearly frightened of the man, certain that the Devil himself had come for Mary's soul. The black van, the black clothes, and those haunting black eyes made more than a few in the crowd nervous.

Once inside the clinic, the mysterious visitor moved past the reception desk and turned down the hall toward Mary's room without hesitation, as if he was as familiar with the facility as the staff.

Dr. Pierce and the head nurse were standing outside Mary's room when the man approached.

"Can I help you, sir?" asked the nurse.

In a low but authoritative voice, he replied, "I've come to see Mary Thorton." Having looked the visitor up and down and having found the man not to his liking, Dr. Pierce said, "I'm afraid that's not possible right now. The woman has but a short time to live, and her husband and a reverend are with her right now."

Dr. Pierce states that he will never forget the look the man gave him as he stared him straight in the eye and said, "Yes, I know. That's why I'm here." He then stepped between the doctor and nurse and entered the room. Reverend Graham had placed the emotionally shattered Paul Thorton in a chair near the bed, where he sat with his head in his hands.

Startled by the sudden appearance of the visitor, Reverend Graham stepped in front of him. "Sir, this is not a good time for visitors. This man's wife is about to depart this life. Are you a member of the family?"

There was a pause. The reverend saw the man staring at the still form of Mary on the bed. "No. I'm not a member of the family, Reverend Graham. I am a man of God, just as you are."

The reverend was momentarily stunned. At no time had he given this man his name. "Do I know you, sir?" asked the pastor.

Moving to the side of Mary's bed, the man did not bother to look up as he answered, "No, Reverend Graham. We have never met."

"May I ask your name, sir?"

"Strange," came the reply.

"Excuse me?" said Graham.

"Reverend Strange is my name."

For some reason that Reverend Graham still cannot explain, the man's name sent a chill down his spine.

"Can I ask why you are here?"

Reverend Strange stood directly over Mary now, and without taking his eyes off her, he answered, "I was on my way to my new church in El Paso when God told me to come here—told me that this woman needed my help."

Paul had regained his composure and rose to stand beside Reverend Graham. Dr. Pierce and the nurse stood in the doorway, watching the mysterious man's every move.

Reverend Strange reached out with his right hand and without hesitation placed it in the center of Mary Thorton's chest. This sudden movement brought a reaction from both Paul and the doctor. As they moved forward, Paul shouted, "Just what do you think you're doing? You can't—"

Before either man could advance another step, Reverend Strange raised his left hand, palm open and up, at Paul and the doctor. Both men were stopped dead.

Then in a low voice, Reverend Strange said, "Please, Mr. Thorton, if you value this woman's life, please put aside your rage and join me in prayer."

With his eyes closed, Reverend Strange began to pray silently. No one in the room could hear the words, but they saw his lips moving, and a sudden glow seemed to warm the room. His hand then moved to Mary's head, and the mysterious reverend continued to pray. In a few minutes, the glow faded from the room, and Reverend Strange was finished. Moving away from the bed, he nodded to Paul and for a fleeting second smiled. Then, without a word, he walked out of the room.

Paul Thorton cannot explain what happened the moment he saw that smile. It was as if his every fear was suddenly lifted from his soul and he knew that Mary was going to be all right. He rushed out into the hall to thank this mysterious man, but it was too late. The black van was just pulling away from the curb.

For a full half hour after the Reverend Strange had departed, nothing changed except Paul's attitude. Then, just as the doctor was about to criticize the Reverend Strange's actions, the heart monitor equipment began to register an ever stronger heartbeat. Dr. Pierce was amazed at the sudden change in the instrument readings.

As he was taking Mary's pulse, she suddenly opened her eyes. The contracted muscles of her face had returned to normal, and her contorted left hand now appeared perfectly fine as she reached out to grasp her husband's trembling hand.

"Can . . . can you hear me, Mary?" asked the doctor.

Smiling her famous smile, Mary replied, "Of course I can, Richard. Just what am I doing here anyway?"

Everyone in the room was stunned. She had no recollection of her ordeal or of how close she had come to death.

"You . . . you had a very bad stroke, Mary," whispered Paul.

Squeezing his hand tightly, she continued to smile. "Now, really, Paul. Do I sound like someone that had a stroke? A little headache, maybe, but goodness, it's not bad enough to warrant all these gadgets."

The following morning, Mary Thorton returned home. Dr. Pierce could find absolutely nothing wrong with her. As a matter of fact, all of his tests showed that if anything, Mary Thorton was as healthy as a woman in her thirties.

Paul and Mary are still as active in the church and the community as ever. The only thing that has changed is that visits from the kids and grandchildren are more frequent.

As for Dr. Pierce, he has never been able to explain the events of that night in his clinic. Medically, Mary Thorton should have died that night. He still keeps all Mary's records and on occasion goes over them again, thinking that perhaps he may have missed something, but each time the records tell the same story.

Reverend Graham has spent the last two years contacting every church in Texas in the hope of locating the mysterious man who spoke with him that night. But to this date, no trace of the man in black and his Chevy van has ever been found. One piece of information that he discovered early on has convinced Reverend Graham that he will never find the mysterious man who called himself Reverend Strange.

It seems that on the night of Mary's miraculous recovery, the Texas Highway Patrol was searching for a late-model black Chevy van wanted in connection with the robbery of a convenience store in a town thirty miles east of Advil. The search covered a hundred-mile radius, and roadblocks were established at every junction. By daylight, the van and its three young occupants had been captured forty miles north of Advil. Reports show that no other black Chevy van was seen or stopped that night. So just what did happen to Reverend Strange and his unforgettable van?

I, for one, have to agree with Mary Thorton. When I asked her where she thought the mysterious reverend might be, she gave me a wonderful smile and a wink, saying simply, "James, you can be sure that wherever Reverend Strange may be, God is riding shotgun in that black Chevy van."

## BRUCE'S STORY

Forty-three-year-old Bruce Holman worked for a large bottling company in Charlotte, North Carolina. Bruce was a strapping bull of a man with arms like a pro football player's. The size and strength of those arms came from snatching up cases of bottles, one in each hand, and swinging them up into the cargo compartments of his delivery truck in preparation for his daily route. Bruce liked his job and had worked for the company for twenty-five years.

Remarkably, over that period of twenty-five years, Bruce missed only two days because of illness. It was an impeccable record, which had never been equaled. Company commendations for his dedication to the organization cover the walls of his den at home. Countless times management had offered him various jobs with higher pay, but those offers all involved a desk job in the front office, something Bruce had absolutely no desire for. He credited the hard work of a route driver with keeping him healthy and fit all those years. Reluctantly accepting his wishes, his company gave him substantial raises over the years as a way of expressing its appreciation. For Bruce Holman, that was recognition enough.

It was in the early fall of 1994 that Bruce's illness began. It started with what seemed to be an innocent hacking cough. Bruce wasn't in the least worried about it at first. He was a smoker and knew that he had been smoking way too much lately. He figured cutting back on the cigarettes and taking cough drops would take care of the problem. But it didn't. The cough grew worse. Bruce quit smoking altogether. He was now taking a bottle of cough syrup to work every day, dosing himself at regular intervals. That seemed to work for a while, but the continual use of the medicine made him feel tired all the time. Soon the coughing spells became increasingly frequent and much more severe.

One night in October, Bruce came home from work feeling miserable. He rushed to the bathroom and was sick for a full ten minutes. He was left totally exhausted. He was feverish, and his chest was sore and ached from the hours of coughing. When he saw the worried look on the face of his wife, Judy, he took her hand and tried to reassure her that everything would be fine.

"Guess it's just a little bronchitis. Nothing to worry about. Okay?"

Judy managed a meager smile then helped her husband to bed. As she was tucking the covers in around him, Bruce said, "You better call the plant and tell them I'll be out for a few days until I whip this thing."

The words sent a chill down Judy's spine. She realized that Bruce's problem was worse than he wanted to admit. For twenty-five years she had watched this giant of a man trek to his truck through snow, sleet, and freezing rain when he had been beset by severe flu. This had to be serious for him to miss a single day, let alone more than one. The worry quickly returned to her face, but Bruce didn't see it this time. He was already fast asleep from pure exhaustion.

Bruce's few days off turned into a week, during which Judy whipped up every concoction she could think of and then turned to herbal medicine books for some new ones. By the end of the week, her efforts appeared to be paying off. Bruce was clearly feeling better. By the time he went to work the following Monday, he believed he had the problem whipped. But Bruce was far from being well.

Three weeks passed. Then Bruce came home in the middle of the day—something he had never done in twenty-five years. He was so sick he could barely stand. He went to bed with a high fever. At 7 P.M. he suffered a violent chill, his teeth chattered, and he shook all over. In spite of an electric blanket and heating pads that Judy placed all around him, Bruce remained in the grip of the chill until well after four in the morning.

Enough was enough. Judy knew how set Bruce was against doctors, but this had gone on far too long to be a cold or the flu or even bronchitis. Something had to be done. With the help of a neighbor, Judy managed to get Bruce into the car and took him to the Emergency Room of the hospital. After a complete examination, the doctor on duty diagnosed Bruce's illness as viral pneumonia. For the next month, he was treated for this illness, but his condition only continued to grow worse.

Each afternoon, Bruce Holman would watch fearfully as the hands on the clock would crawl toward six o'clock. He had learned to dread that hour, for he knew all too well what lay in store for him. With devastating regularity, the pattern continued to repeat itself night after night. Between six and seven o'clock, he would be seized with a hard chill, so violent that the entire bed would shake and the chattering of his teeth could be heard in the other room. After the chills began, he would start to sweat then chill again throughout the night until five in the morning. He would finally fall into a deep sleep that would last perhaps two hours or so, when he would suddenly be awakened by a severe coughing spell. Whether the chill or the sweating or the coughing was most distressing would be difficult to say.

When the chill broke, Bruce's body would be bathed in perspiration and his bed would be soaked. Judy would often have to change the bed as many as four times in one night. These severe sweats so weakened Bruce that his doctor began to express grave concern for his patient. Then one night, the most frightening symptom of all began to appear: Each time Bruce coughed in the grip of the chill, he would find himself unable to breathe, and no medication relieved this terrifying shortage of breath.

By the end of one month, prostrate from the alternating chills and sweating, exhausted by continual coughing, suffering increased difficulty in breathing and a loss of over fifty pounds, Bruce was now in serious condition. His doctor knew that viral pneumonia alone was not sufficient to explain the effects of his patient's illness. He would have to be moved to the hospital again.

Over the next three weeks, Bruce was subjected to tests for everything from malaria to tuberculosis to cancer. All the tests proved negative, and his ordeal continued.

Finally, a doctor from a hospital in Greensboro questioned Bruce closely about the nature of his work before he was stricken with his illness. This physician discovered that the area where Bruce always loaded his truck was located only a few yards from the bottle sterilization section, building where alkali was mixed with water in the bottle washer for sterilization purposes. It was this doctor's theory that over the years Bruce must have inhaled vast quantities of the fumes from the mixture, which were circulated around the vicinity of his truck by a small exhaust fan set in the side wall of the sterilization building. The doctor suspected lung damage from the alkali and recommended that Bruce be flown to the Lung Institute.

Sure enough, the Institute's tests proved the doctor to be correct. Bruce's lungs were indeed badly burned from the gradual inhalation of the fumes from the bottle washer mixture. His illness was finally diagnosed as emphysema and bronchial asthma.

Although many people have heard of emphysema, few people realize that it is more prevalent than lung cancer and T.B. combined. It is difficult to diagnose and is more often than not misdiagnosed as pneumonia or bronchitis.

With emphysema, the lungs fill up with air that the patient cannot exhale. Eventually, the overextended lungs lose their elasticity. The diaphragm, which moves freely up and down during the normal breathing process, gradually flattens and becomes immobile. The normal person at rest breathes about fourteen times a minute, while victims of emphysema breathe up to thirty times a minute and still cannot get enough oxygen. They suffer from chronic and generalized oxygen deficiency, and their muscles weaken from lack of oxygen and little use until the least activity involves almost superhuman effort.

Another characteristic of the disease is patients' inability, no matter how hard they cough, to expel the mucus that troubles them. As they strain to cough this heavy fluid up, with little or no success, the bronchial passageways rupture. Swollen and scarred, the passageways thicken and become increasingly narrow.

There is no known medical cure for emphysema, only palliative treatment that in some cases helps and in others does not. All its victims, regardless of treatment, are doomed to live out their lives fighting a constant battle against breathlessness.

The extent of disability depends upon the damage done to the lungs. According to the doctors who treated Bruce Holman, his case was both severe and permanent. His incapacitation was considered virtually total in every way. Their only solution for Bruce was for him to rely on a mask and a bottle of oxygen when the breathing became too severe, but as for a permanent cure, there was none. The alkali had combined with years of smoking. The damage to Bruce's lungs was so severe that even a lung transplant was ruled out. The waiting list was a long one, and few if any of the doctors gave Bruce that long to live.

Devastated by the news, Judy took her husband home to care for him as best she could. He still suffered his battles with the chills, but the oxygen bottle did help with the battle for breath. One night, following a rough bout with the chills and fever, Judy knelt beside her husband's bed and held his hand and prayed for God to intervene. Although not a totally religious man, Bruce had been a good husband and a kind father to their children. Judy remained at Bruce's bedside until morning, constantly praying. She did the same the next night and every night for a week, but Bruce did not seem to improve. Perhaps she needed more help, thought Judy.

The following week, she enlisted the aid of the Reverend Charles Osgood, pastor of the First Methodist church, a church that Judy and her children had attended for years. Bruce had attended only a few times, and then only because his wife insisted that not doing so would make a bad impression on the children.

On his first visit, Judy informed the pastor that Bruce was a good man and believed in God, but that he had never really thought much about religion or prayer. As far as she knew, Bruce had never prayed for anything in his life. They conferred for a few minutes in the living room, then Judy led the pastor to Bruce's room. Judy could tell that Bruce was not comfortable with their visitor, but he greeted the man with a friendly smile and a warm handshake.

For more than an hour they discussed Bruce's condition, his belief in the power of God, and the power of prayer. All in all, it was a very pleasant visit. As he was leaving, Reverend Osgood asked Bruce if next time he might bring along some members of the church's prayer group to talk with him and conduct a service of the laying of hands as they prayed for him. Caught a little off guard by this, Bruce wasn't sure what to say. But having spent an hour with this man of God, and feeling more at ease than he had in months, Bruce could see no harm in it, if that was what they wanted to do. He still didn't believe anything could come of it, but at this point, he was willing to try anything.

"Why, sure, Reverend. If you think it'll do any good, I'd be glad to have them here." Those words brought a smile to his wife's beautiful face, a smile that had been missing for a long, long time.

Two nights later, Reverend Osgood and his prayer group arrived. Although he would never admit it, Bruce Holman was as nervous as a cat at a dog convention. Introductions were made all around, then the group formed a circle around Bruce's bed. Kneeling down, the group reached out and placed their hands on Bruce's body, and the praying began. Bruce lay with his eyes closed and silently said the Lord's Prayer, the only prayer he knew. After thirty minutes, Pastor Osgood ended the prayer session, and the group departed.

Bruce waited to see if anything would happen, but nothing changed. As a matter of fact, that night was one of the worse nights he'd ever had. By morning, he was totally exhausted and more than a little disappointed.

Equally exhausted, Judy noticed that Bruce's supply of medication was almost gone. She would have to replace it before Bruce woke up. Certain that he would sleep all morning, Judy left a note by his bed just in case and headed for the drugstore.

Normally, following a rough night, Bruce would sleep until late in the afternoon, but this was not to be a normal day for Bruce Holman. Less than ten minutes after Judy had left, Bruce suddenly sat up straight in bed, fully awake. The words Reverend Osgood had spoken that first night they met kept repeating themselves in his head. "You have only to believe and call upon the Lord with all your heart, and he will hear your prayer."

With tears streaming down his face, Bruce Holman knew in his heart that this was the time to take God at his word—"By my stripes you are healed"—so he simply looked up and asked with all his heart for God to heal him as he had healed so many others.

He immediately felt a great spreading warmth in his chest and then became deathly sick. He was suddenly gripped by fear but then thought, "Don't be afraid of God. This is what you ask of him."

Struggling from his bed, Bruce made his way to the bathroom. Leaning on the sink for support, he fought to catch his breath. Then suddenly, there came from his mouth the equivalent of a water glass full of heavy, clear fluid. The experience nearly took the big man to his knees. When he raised his head, Bruce Holman took his first deep breath in nearly two years. For a full five minutes, he did nothing but stand before the mirror and cry while breathing as normally as he ever had and giving thanks to God, Reverend Osgood, and the prayer group.

When Judy returned home, she saw that he wasn't in his bed, but his bottle of oxygen was still there. Bruce couldn't walk from one room to the other without it. Sudden panic sent her searching throughout the house for Bruce. But he was nowhere to be found.

Then she heard what she thought was a lawn mower in the backyard. Rushing to the back door, she was stunned to see Bruce in a T-shirt and shorts, mowing their lawn, just as he had always done before the illness.

Seeing his loving wife, he shut off the mower and like an eighteen-year-old boy, raced across the lawn and grabbed her up in his arms and began to twirl her about, all the time saying, "God did it, Judy. I just had to ask him myself. Isn't the Lord God great!"

Today, Bruce and Judy Holman live very comfortably in a new home outside Charlotte. The company for which Bruce had worked so long realized its responsibility for the suffering this man had gone through and its obligation. Without lawyers or courts, the company took it upon itself to provide the Holmans with a financial arrangement that will guarantee them a comfortable retirement and insure that their grandchildren will not have to worry about college.

As for the doctors, numerous tests have left them totally amazed by Bruce's condition. All together they have attested to the fact that Bruce's lungs are perfect. They cannot even find the traces of nicotine that would normally exist in a person who has smoked for a year, let alone twenty years.

Bruce owns a landscaping business now, and although he has fifteen employees, he still gets out there with them, planting trees, mowing lawns, and laying rolls of Bermuda grass for new lawns.

He and Judy attend church on a regular basis, and Bruce is always telling anyone who will listen, "It is when active faith dares to believe God to the point of action that something has got to happen. Just take God at his word, and miracles will happen."

# MICHAEL'S STORY

Karen Rhodes can still remember the day that she thought her world was about to come to an end. That moment came the afternoon that Dr. Earl Weatherby received the results of a series of tests that he had conducted on her twelve-year-old-son, Michael.

It was 3 P.M. on June 9, 1993. Karen was in Dr. Weatherby's office. Looking up from the thick medical file lying before him, the doctor shook his head and in a low voice filled with both sorrow and compassion for this thirty-two-year-old single mother, he informed her that her son, Michael, was dying, and, regrettably, there was nothing they could do to prevent it. His condition had deteriorated at such a rapid rate that the usual surgery would do little or no good and would only subject the child to unnecessary pain and suffering.

Karen Rhodes slumped back in her chair. Her lower lip quivered slightly. Her attempt at playing the unshakable rock totally disintegrated as she tried to imagine life without her child. As the doctor's words resounded through her head, Karen Rhodes's body began to shake, and she broke into tears.

Michael had been diagnosed with a brain tumor. Adding to Karen's burden was the knowledge that had Michael been seen by a specialist early on, there might have been a chance to stop the progression of the disease, but now it was too late. For this Karen blamed herself. Things had been tough, and she had to work two jobs to make ends meet. When she wasn't working, she was cleaning house, washing clothes, and trying to sleep whenever she could. When Michael had first mentioned the headaches, she had given him aspirins and told him he'd get better. But he never did. Knowing how hard his mother worked for them and how tight money was, Michael didn't tell his mother how bad the headaches really were. He'd take his aspirins and go to bed with his pain.

One day she had come home and found Michael unconscious on the floor. That was a month ago. Now Karen blamed herself for what had happened to her son. The doctor's prognosis and her guilt were more than she could stand.

Dr. Weatherby moved to Karen's side and placed a caring hand on her shoulder in an attempt to comfort the sobbing mother. "Lord knows, Karen, if I thought there was even the slightest chance, I'd be operating right now. But . . . that's not the case. I'm sorry, Karen."

The kindly doctor's words only unleashed another wave of muffled sobs and a steady stream of tears. Dr. Weatherby had never felt so totally helpless. Not knowing what else he could say, he patted her shoulder gently then left his office, quietly closing the door behind him.

The nurse and receptionist both heard Karen crying as the physician came out of the room. "Let that young lady remain in my office as long as she wants. I'll see my other patients in the exam room. No one is to enter my office until she leaves."

"Should I go in to be with her?" asked the nurse.

"No, I think it's best that she be by herself for now."

The receptionist shook her head sadly. "There's no hope at all, Doctor?" she asked.

"No, I'm afraid not," said Weatherby with a tear in his eye. "If we had seen him months ago—maybe. But now, I'd estimate that it will only be a matter of days before he's gone."

Karen remained in the doctor's office for nearly an hour before she managed to pull herself together enough to leave. She nodded to the receptionist as she left and told her to thank the doctor for his kindness.

As Karen slid in behind the wheel of her car she noticed Michael's Little League baseball cap lying on the backseat. A surge of emotion swept over her, but she fought back the tears. She had already cried more than she thought humanly possible. No, more tears would not solve anything. But what was she going to do? Everyone she had talked to on this day had said the same thing. "It's over—there's nothing anyone can do." "Your son is going to die." "Oh, the poor thing—her son's dying." All those words were racing through her mind and were as painful as a stake being driven through her heart.

What should she do first? What about Michael's father? She should let him know what was happening to his son. But how? He had deserted them when Michael was only three. Karen had raised their son alone. No, that wouldn't work either. She had no idea where the father was now or if he would even care enough to return to Dallas to see his son one last time.

Sitting alone in her car, turning the ball cap slowly in her small hands, Karen felt the tears welling up again. There was no one to turn to. Her parents had been killed in an auto accident on Michael's second birthday. Her brother, Mark, had been killed in the Gulf War. And her only real friend, Carolyn, Mark's wife, had taken their children and moved back to Seattle. No, there was no family she could turn to in this time of need, no one to lean on for strength and courage. For the last nine years it had been just her and Michael. Now even he was being taken away from her.

Karen wasn't sure how long she sat in the parking lot, but it was dark by the time she smoked her third cigarette. There was no smoking in the hospital. Karen was going to quit, but right now was not the time. Her nerves needed all the help they could get. Locking the car, she walked slowly back to the hospital entrance.

Still clutching Michael's hat in her hands, she entered the lobby and made the familiar trek past the front desk to the elevators. While she pressed the button and waited, she noticed a young couple coming out of the double doors of the chapel, which was located a short distance from the elevators. As they passed Karen, it was obvious from their eyes that they had been crying, whether from joy or sadness, Karen could not be sure. The elevator doors opened, but Karen's eyes were still fixed on the chapel doors.

Michael had been in this hospital for a month, and not once had she even thought of entering that room. For Karen, religion and God had begun to fade from her life when her parents had been killed by a drunk driver. She had called upon God for answers. Why? Why them? But there were no answers. When her husband deserted her, she again called upon God for answers, but none came. Standing in the rain and watching her only brother's coffin being lowered into the cold ground at Arlington Cemetery marked the final time Karen had called upon God for anything. She had come to believe that asking anything of God was a total waste of time. Now that same God who had ignored her so many times was about to take away the only thing she had left. What kind of God was that?

The elevator doors opened then closed again, but Karen was still standing there staring at the chapel doors. But why? She had given up on asking God for anything. Why should this time be any different? Still, there seemed to be something pushing her, forcing her toward the chapel. Before she realized it, she was standing before the double doors and reaching out for the highly polished handles. Pulling the doors open, she walked inside. The lighting was soft but dim. She made her way down to the front. Before her stood a ten-foot cross with the figure of Jesus crucified. Flowers abounded along the walls, and the sounds of soft, peaceful music filled the room.

Karen found herself drawn to the front pew, where she lowered herself onto the bench, her eyes never leaving the face of the Jesus before her. She sat staring in silence for a long time. What was she doing here? Three times she had called upon God. Three times she had prayed for some sense of understanding, some sign or feeling of inner peace that would ease the grief of those terrible times. And three times she had received nothing for her efforts. God did not have time for her. Yet here she sat, gazing upon a statue of the Son of God crucified. The feeling of hopelessness returned. Alone and exhausted, Karen lowered her weary head into her hands and asked, "Oh, God—why can't you help me—just this once?"

"He did," said a gentle voice from behind her.

Karen straightened suddenly. Startled, she turned to face a well-dressed young man in his early twenties.

"Excuse me," she said.

The young man first apologized for having startled her, then went on to explain that the statue before them represented the ultimate example of God's love for all. "What of greater value could God have given to save us all?" he asked.

Karen stared at the statue for a long moment, then suddenly was filled with shame. How could she have allowed herself to turn away from God? Overcome by grief, she broke down and began to weep. The young man moved forward. Sitting beside her, he comforted her until she stopped crying.

For the next thirty minutes, they sat and discussed Michael's illness and her fears. The young man's name was Daniel Foreman. He was the senior leader of a prayer group from a church called the Evangelistic Temple. They had come to the hospital to pray for a member of their group who had been in an accident the previous night. An intelligent and highly observant young man, Daniel could see immediately that Karen had lost all hope for her son as well as her faith in God.

Had she prayed for Michael? he asked.

No, she replied. God was not interested enough in her prayers.

Daniel shook his head sadly. "Well, maybe if we both try, we can get his attention. Come on."

Taking her hand, he led her to within a few feet of the cross. They knelt together. Daniel began to pray. Karen hesitated for a moment, then found herself praying as she had never prayed before. First, for forgiveness for having lost her way to God. Second, in thanks for his having given his only Son to save the world. Third, she asked that God find the mercy in his heart to save her only son. They prayed for ten minutes.

When they finally rose to their feet, Karen felt a sudden rush of relief race through her body. It was as if the burdens of the last ten years had been lifted from her. For the first time since she could remember, she actually felt good.

Together Karen and her newfound friend left the chapel.

"What room is Michael in?" asked Daniel.

"405."

"Go to your son now. I'll check on my friend then join you there."

Karen nodded. As she stood in the elevator watching Daniel walk away, she offered a silent "Thank you, God" for having brought this young man into her life at this moment.

Entering Michael's room, Karen moved to the bedside of her young son. Surrounded by a host of beeping monitors, wires, and tubes, he looked so helpless. Placing her hand on his head, she closed her eyes and began to pray once more for the life of her son. Her voice was suddenly joined by others. Opening her eyes, Karen saw Daniel standing across from her, his hand on Michael's chest, his eyes closed. He too was praying. To his left and right were three young women and three young men, all about the same age as Daniel. They had formed a circle around Michael's bed, and each had a hand touching her son. Their eyes closed, they prayed for the life of this boy.

The group prayed over Michael for nearly an hour. By the time they left the room,

Karen's spirits were uplifted. That night, she left her son's room feeling that something had happened. She didn't know what or how. It was just a feeling that seemed to surge through her very soul. It was hope rekindled.

In the hall, Daniel made the introductions, and the group talked for a while. Giving her encouragement for Michael's recovery, they left for the night with the promise that they would return at the same time the following night. Thanking them all, Karen returned to Michael's room and took her familiar place in the small chair beside his bed. Holding his hand in hers, Karen fell asleep next to Michael, just as she had every night for the last month.

For the next three nights, Daniel and his group returned to Michael's bedside and, with the laying on of hands, prayed for the boy. Each night, before they left, they told Karen not to give up hope. She always smiled and told them not to worry. She now knew that God was with Michael and if it was his will, her son would live.

On the fifth day, Dr. Weatherby came by to check on Michael, just as he had done every morning. It was early morning. When he entered the room, he saw Karen sleeping, her son's hand in hers. He tried not to wake her. As he started to leave the room, he noticed the readings on the cranial monitor. They were rising. That could only mean brain activity, and the numbers were increasing as he stood there. But how could this be? This boy was supposed to be dying. He had been comatose for more than four weeks. With the rapid spread of the tumor, these numbers should be decreasing, not rising.

All thought of Karen's rest forgotten, Dr. Weatherby suddenly called at the top of his voice, "Nurse—get in here!"

The booming voice startled Karen. She instantly came to her feet. Still not quite awake, she rubbed at her eyes as she asked, "What . . . what is it? Is something wrong with Michael? What's happened?"

Dr. Weatherby stood across the room, Michael's chart in his hands, the head nurse by his side. "Unbelievable!" he muttered as his eyes went from the chart to the monitor and back again. "Nurse. Are these recorded readings correct?" The nurse assured him that they were. "Unbelievable," he whispered again.

"What is it, Doctor?" asked Karen, unable to hide the panic raising in her voice.

"It's wonderful is what it is," said the doctor as he moved to Michael's bedside and exposed the boy's chest to listen to his heartbeat. He checked his eyes. He then rattled off the names of two drugs that he wanted administered through Michael's IV immediately. Karen wasn't sure whether to be excited or horrified at the rapid series of events that was going on in the room.

Two nurses rushed into the room with the medication ordered. The doctor stepped over to Karen and with a joyous smile on his face placed his hands on her arms.

"Karen, I don't profess to know how or why this has happened. I've heard about you and your friends praying every night for Michael. Maybe that's it. I just don't know. But one thing is certain. Your son is showing signs of a remarkable recovery from his coma. If I'm right, and the medication I just ordered works as I believe it will, Michael should be waking up in the next thirty to forty-five minutes."

Karen had to sit down. This was all too much for her. Less than a week ago, Michael had been pronounced as good as dead. Now, thanks to a gracious God, she was on the verge of having her son returned to her. Just as startling to her was the realization that God had heard her plea and she was about to receive the sign that she had sought so many times before.

The following forty-five minutes were the longest in Karen's life. As the minutes passed, the room began to fill with doctors and nurses, all those who had worked with Michael since his arrival at the hospital. When Karen lowered her head and began to repeat the Lord's Prayer, every person in the room bowed their heads and joined her in reciting the words.

Minutes after they finished their prayer,

young Michael Rhodes opened his eyes for the first time in more than a month. His eyelids fluttered a few times, then his eyes focused on his mother.

Then, speaking as if he had just awakened from an afternoon nap, he said, "Hi, Mom. Why are you crying?"

Karen leaned over the bed and hugged the son she had feared lost. "Mama's just happy, honey. So very happy."

Needless to say, there was not a dry eye in the room.

Over the next few hours, Dr. Weatherby had a complete series of X rays and a CAT scan run on Michael. At four in the afternoon, he sat in his lab with the results of the X rays and the scan before him. Not one showed any sign of cancer or tumors. They were pictures of a normal twelve-year-old boy. Another doctor in the room removed four of the X rays from the light board and replaced them with four X rays that had been taken within hours of Michael's admittance to the hospital one month earlier. There, plain as day, was a black spot the size of a silver dollar. A first-year intern could have diagnosed these X rays as a brain tumor. But now it was gone without a trace.

Both doctors looked from one set of X rays to the other, then back again.

"What do you think?" asked Dr. Weatherby. "Any explanation?"

His fellow doctor shook his head. "No, sir. None at all. But if anyone ever asks me if I believe in prayer or miracles, I'm going to have a great story to tell them."

Dr. Weatherby informed an overjoyed Karen that not only had her son successfully regained full consciousness, but all sign of the tumor had totally disappeared. Medically, he could offer no explanation. But as a Christian and true believer, he gave all the credit to God and the prayers offered up in Michael's behalf.

Karen couldn't wait to let Daniel and his friends know of Michael's total recovery. That night, when they arrived at the hospital, Karen was waiting for them. At hearing the news of Michael's miracle, they all went to the chapel and gave thanks to the true physician for Michael's healing.

In August of 1998, Michael Rhodes will be a senior in high school. He has never had anything worse than the common cold or the flu since his recovery in 1993. A strong and healthy young man with outstanding athletic ability, he is being pursued by a number of colleges for scholarships in both football and basketball.

Karen met the man of her dreams in 1996 and remarried. She and Michael are living happily with their new husband and father in Miami, Florida, where Daniel Foreman and his friends are always welcome guests.

## MAGGIE'S MIRACLE

Sharon Metcalf can still remember the day her father called long distance to tell her that her mother had been diagnosed with cancer. It was Mother's Day, 1989.

Sharon was twenty years old at the time and a student at Oklahoma University. Normally she would have been home for the summer break, but she had opted for summer classes to pick up some extra credits and for work with her student Christian group, which was involved in the handicapped children's summer program. The news about her mother would change all those plans.

Sharon told her father she would pack immediately and be on her way home to Tulsa by that afternoon. After she hung up the phone, she wandered about the apartment in a state of near shock. No matter how hard she tried, she just couldn't get herself organized. In frustration, she sat down on the edge of her bed and tried to sort it all out.

Sharon couldn't imagine her mother being ill, let alone having a deadly disease like cancer. She could count on one hand the number of times she had seen her mother sick. It just didn't happen. Yet now this wonderful woman, who had spent nearly all her life caring for a husband and three kids, a woman who had cared for them all when they were sick or hurt or depressed, this woman was now facing a battle for her life. And it was a battle she had little or no chance of winning. The seemingly invincible Maggie Metcalf had been diagnosed with cancer of the liver.

Christy Turner, Sharon's roommate, came through the door about the time that Sharon broke down and began to cry. Going to her friend's side, Christy put her arms around her and asked what was wrong. The news was equally shocking to Christy. She often went home with Sharon for the weekend, and Maggie had become like a second mother to her.

They both cried for a while, holding each other close, each trying to comfort the other. Finally, wiping the tears away, Christy helped Sharon pack and carry her things to the car. She wanted to go with Sharon, but that wasn't possible. Christy's parents were arriving that night from Oakland, California, to spend a week with their daughter. But Christy promised that the minute they were gone, she would be on her way to Tulsa.

Before she drove away, Sharon asked that Christy and the kids in the Christian group please remember her mother at their group prayer sessions. Christy assured her that they would.

Sharon had made the trip from Norman to Tulsa more times than she could count, but on this day the drive seemed to be taking forever. On two occasions, she had to pull off the road, tears having welled up in her eyes, obscuring the road ahead. She would have a good cry, then, after composing herself, continue on her way.

She still couldn't believe it. Cancer! And liver cancer at that. She wasn't up on the latest cures or treatments for the disease. As a matter of fact, she was surprised at how little she did knew about it. One thing she did know: When a person's liver no longer functioned, that person was dead.

It was night by the time she pulled into the driveway of her home. There were a number of cars parked in front of the house. She recognized one of them. It belonged to her sister, Terry. She was glad her elder sister was already there. Now, if only her brother Jimmy had been there. But she knew that wasn't possible. Jimmy was a marine and was serving somewhere in the Middle East. She knew her father, a former marine himself, would not send for him until Mom became critical.

Her father and Terry met her at the door. Sharon hugged them both. While her father gathered her things from the car, Terry took her into the living room. There, sitting in her favorite rocker, was her mother. Next to her on the couch was Pastor Kennel of the First Methodist church, and beside him sat Sister Katherine from Saint Mary's Church, a close friend of the family.

Hurrying to her mother's side, Sharon knelt down and threw her arms around Maggie and hugged her as never before. "Oh, Mama," she cried, "I love you so much."

At that moment, Sharon became aware of a familiar touch—her mother's hand gently patting the back of her head, just as she had for twenty years.

"Now, now, honey," said her mother softly, "I'm okay. Don't you be hiding those pretty blue eyes with all those tears."

The words brought back a flood of memories for Sharon. They were the same words her mother used whenever she had hurt herself riding her bike or had taken a fall on her skates. They had held special meaning when she had suffered her first broken heart over the loss of her first love at age thirteen.

Terry prepared tea, and everyone talked about anything and everything but Maggie's illness. Sharon couldn't help but notice the haggard, weary look on her mother's face. It was clear that the news had been a shock to many, but for Maggie it had been devastating.

The eyes looked dark, and the normal glow on her cheeks was no longer there.

After an hour or so, Maggie said that she was feeling tired and felt she should go to bed. As Sharon's father moved to the chair to help her mother, Sharon asked, "Mother, could we all hold hands first and have Pastor Kennel and Sister Katherine lead us in a moment of prayer?"

The request drew a stern glare from her father. A strange and surprising silence seemed to fall over the room, as if everyone was waiting for Maggie's approval. Sharon was taken aback by the situation. Her mother was the most religious, churchgoing woman she had ever known. What in the world was going on?

Maggie eased herself back into the rocker and extended her hand to her young daughter. "Of course we can, dear. If that's what you want."

The words stunned Sharon. If that was what *she* wanted!

Taking her mother's hand, she reached out for Terry's with the other. When the circle was completed, Pastor Kennel asked for a blessing upon the family in this time of crisis. Sister Katherine then did the same. As they were praying, Sharon glanced at her mother. She was staring across the room as if she were in another world.

After the pastor and Sister Katherine had left and her father had taken her mother to their bedroom, Sharon cornered Terry in the kitchen.

"Just what was all that about?" she asked, "I haven't had a look like that from Dad since that time I backed into his new truck when I was seventeen."

Terry poured herself a glass of milk and shook her head. "I wish I knew, Sis. Mom's been a lot different ever since Dr. Toben told her about the cancer."

Terry went on to explain that their mother had ridden all the way home from the doctor's office without saying a word. No matter what their father said, she just wouldn't talk. When they got home, she went to her room and went to bed. That was a week ago. Only during the last few days had she been speaking to anyone.

"But why the look from Dad?" Sharon asked.

"Because she doesn't believe in prayer anymore," said her father, who had entered the kitchen. Moving to the table, he sat down and continued, "I'm not so sure she even believes there's a God anymore."

The two daughters joined their obviously depressed father at the table. Reaching out and clutching each daughter's hand, he squeezed them tightly as he said, "In the forty years I've been with your mom, I've never seen her give up on anything. But girls, this thing has wiped out just about every belief she's ever had. It's going to take all of us to keep her going."

Chester Metcalf went on to explain how this had all started. Three months earlier, Maggie had been having problems with her kidneys, along with sharp pains in her lower abdomen. A trip to the family physician, Dr. Toben, soon resulted in a wide range of tests that required three separate trips to the hospital over a four-day period. Both Chester and Maggie knew something was wrong when the doctor asked that Maggie return to the hospital for more tests.

One week later, the doctor called. He needed to see them in his office as soon as possible. It was then that they had received the bad news. He told them up front that the odds of surviving this type of cancer were slim to none. Dr. Toben had never been one to pull punches. Nevertheless, he wanted Maggie to begin treatment immediately.

But their mother had refused. What was the use? When she began to open up to her husband, she insisted that he not tell the kids about her cancer. It was a promise he had kept until she had started to show signs of deep depression, a sense of hopelessness that began to affect him as well. That was when he knew it was time to call in reinforcements. He called

Pastor Kennel and Sister Katherine immediately after he called his daughters.

That night, around the table, three members of the Metcalf family vowed that they would do whatever it took to preserve Maggie's life for as long as possible and restore her faith in a God they knew she truly did love.

For the next five days, Maggie was bombarded with pleas, tears, hugs, and prayers not only by Chester, Terry, and Sharon but by Sister Katherine and Pastor Kennel, who also enlisted the aid of practically every member of the Methodist church. More than a hundred cards arrived containing quotes from the Bible about God's healing miracles and his eternal love for all who would have faith in him. By the time Dr. Toben called on the sixth day to make his own impassioned plea, Maggie had no choice but to give in. She agreed to go to the hospital. Dr. Toben would have everything ready for her to be admitted. They would start her treatment the next morning.

Sharon thought they had won a victory over this headstrong woman by getting her admitted to the hospital, but after only a few days of treatment, Sharon began to wonder if they had done the right thing. Maggie looked worse now than she had at home. There were dark circles under her eyes, eyes that seemed to have little life left in them. Her skin was beginning to take on a yellowish hue, a sure sign that her liver was beginning to fail. Dr. Toben was doing all he could, but from the test results, it was apparent that they had waited too long. Two other physicians were consulted. Their tests confirmed Dr. Toben's findings. They gave Maggie less than three months to live. Their conclusions were relayed to the family by Dr. Toben, who confessed that other than providing medication for the pain, there was nothing more they could do.

It was a somber group that greeted Christy as she entered Maggie's room. She was shocked to see Maggie's condition; the dark-set eyes, the weight loss that was clearly apparent in her face, and the yellow tint of her skin. Sharon took Christy aside and told her the doctor's diagnosis.

Had they tried everything? asked Christy. Sharon assured her they had.

"What about prayer?" Christy asked.

"Of course, we've prayed for her," replied Sharon.

"How often? And how many?"

Sharon began to feel as though she were being interrogated by the FBI. "We all do at different times, I suppose. Why?"

"That's no good, Sharon. We've got to organize an around-the-clock prayer vigil for your mom. The doctors have done all they can. Now we have to go to the main man with this problem. I'll be back soon."

Sharon watched her friend race from the room. What was she up to?

That night, the Metcalf family was surprised to see Christy and the entire Christian Group arrive, Bibles in hand. There were no less than fourteen people in the room when Dr. Toben arrived to make a final check on Maggie before going home. When told what they intended to do, Dr. Toben heartily gave his blessing. Mortal man had done all he could. It was time to turn this case over to a higher power. As he was leaving, Pastor Kennel arrived. Christy had called him. A few minutes later, Sister Katherine came through the door. She carried a small red velvet bag in her right hand. It was something she had requested from a special place in France.

Christy organized the students in a circle around the bed with Pastor Kennel at the head of the bed and Sister Katherine at the foot. Maggie, heavy-eyed from the painkillers she was being given, tried to smile in appreciation of their efforts.

One by one the students placed a hand on Maggie, then each chose a passage from the Bible and read it while the others repeated it word for word. When Sister Katherine's turn came, the nun removed a small vial from the red bag she carried. It was filled with a clear liquid. It was filled with a clear liquid. Raising it into the air, she explained that the vial contained water from the holy shrine at Lourdes, France, site of countless miracles over the years. Blessed by the Bishop of Lourdes, it had been sent to Sister Katherine specifically for Maggie.

Sister Katherine began to pray in Latin as she sprinkled the holy water over Maggie's midsection. Those who could do so echoed her prayer. Around and around the prayer circle continued well into the night. At midnight, the group broke up and went home, vowing to return the following morning at nine to begin again.

True to their word, the circle was formed in the morning, and the prayers continued until noon. That night, they went till midnight again. This continued for three straight days and nights. By the fourth day, Dr. Toben began to notice a slight change in Maggie's color. True, it was a slight change, but a change nonetheless. The entire group became excited at word of the change and renewed its prayers with a new confidence.

By the end of the week, Maggie was fully aware of what was going on around her, and the gentle touches and words of hope began to lift her spirits, renewing her faith in the only one who could heal her. For those in the circle, this renewed faith was the true healing.

By the ninth day, Maggie's color had returned to normal, and the darkness around her eyes had vanished. A new battery of tests was ordered by Dr. Toben, and the results showed a marked improvement in her condition—so much so that he wanted Maggie to consent to exploratory surgery. The tests showed the cancer in remission, but the only way to be certain was to operate. Maggie agreed to the procedure without hesitation.

As Maggie's loved ones and supporters prayed for her in the waiting room, Dr. Toben, assisted by the two physicians he had consulted earlier, began the operation. They had allowed for a period of one to two hours, but once they had begun, that quickly changed. One can only imagine their shock and amazement when they saw that Maggie's liver was as healthy-looking as their own. Not one trace of cancer could be found. All three doctors checked the area a second time to make sure. In little more than thirty minutes, the operation was over. Three days later, Maggie Metcalf returned home, cancer-free and with a renewed faith that could never be challenged again.

Whether it was the prayer circle or the water from Lourdes or both, the fact remains that when medical science had done all it was capable of doing and failed, after the prayer vigil, Maggie began to improve. Dr. Toben gives the credit for Maggie's recovery to a power higher than mortal man. It is a view shared by his two colleagues as well.

Today Maggie is still going strong. No sign of the cancer has ever returned. Sharon is married and has two children of her own, and Christy is still her closest friend. We should all have such friends.

# THE BOYS OF SUMMER

Thirteen-year-old Brett Waddle was the star pitcher for the Omaha Wildcats, and the Wildcats were on their way to a Little League Baseball Championship. They needed to win only one final game. The game was tight, and their opposition, the Outlaws, were coming up to bat for the last time. The Wildcats held a one-run lead. If Brett could strike out these last three batters, the Wildcats could win it all.

The stands were filled to capacity, and sitting right up front were Brett's parents and grandparents, cheering him on with as much enthusiasm as his teammates.

The first batter came to the plate. Brett ignored the butterflies in his stomach and went to work. "Strike one!" resounded the call from the umpire. The crowd in the stands roared its approval.

"Strike two!" Another roar rose from the observers. Brett could feel his confidence building with each cheer from the crowd. "Strike three-you're out!" yelled the umpire.

The ball was passed around the infield, then back to Brett.

"One down and two to go," he whispered to himself as he wiped the sweat from his forehead.

The second Outlaw stepped up to the plate. Brett's first two pitches were low and outside, but Brett came right back with three straight pitches to strike the batter out.

Johnny Majors, one of Brett's closest friends, caught the ball on the pass around and moved to the pitcher's mound from his first base position. Rubbing the ball a couple of times, he handed it to Brett and with a broad smile told his friend, "You're the man, Brett! Two gone—now take this guy out and we've got it all."

"No problem," replied Brett.

The third batter stepped up to the plate. He was the Outlaws' catcher. He was not only the biggest kid on the Outlaws team, but he was also the league's leading hitter, with a batting average of .435. Brett's first pitch caught the outside corner for strike one. The second pitch was fouled off—two strikes. One more strike, and the championship would belong to the Wildcats.

Brett knew he had thrown the wrong pitch the second it left his hand. A fast ball straight down the middle. The batter brought his bat around with all his might, catching the ball solidly. But it didn't go screaming skyward for the outfield fence—instead, it came off the bat like a bullet, a round bullet that streaked straight back at the pitcher with such speed that Brett Waddle had no time to react.

The baseball struck the young pitcher on the right side of the head. The impact was so loud that it could be heard by the outfielders. Brett dropped like a rock, unconscious before he hit the ground.

For a frightening second, a stunned silence fell over the entire park. Even the batter, who had delivered the blow, still stood in the batter's box, as if frozen there by the sickening sound the ball had made when it struck Brett. A scream in the stands from Brett's mother was followed by others from the women in the crowd. "My God! He's dead!" screamed someone. Suddenly, players and people from the stands were rushing for the pitcher's mound.

The Emergency Medical Technicians who had been watching the game from behind the backstop scrambled to their ambulance and were on the field within a minute. Pushing her way through the crowd that had gathered around the injured boy, Denise Hayden, a veteran EMT with ten years' experience, took one look at the enormous swelling that had already deformed the right side of Brett's head and knew they had precious little time to get the boy to the hospital.

Within seconds, the other EMT had the stretcher at the pitcher's mound. Brett was carefully placed on it then rushed to the open doors of the ambulance.

Denise yelled out, "Please get back! Where are the parents? Get in here now. We're leaving. Hurry up!"

Larry and Donna Waddle stepped quickly into the back of the ambulance as Denise shut the doors and yelled to the driver, "Get moving, Jerry! This kid's on the clock!"

Those words sent a chill through the parents, who were themselves still in a state of shock, unable to believe what had happened to their son.

As the ambulance raced off the field and onto the highway, Denise was already on the radio, advising the hospital that they were inbound and giving vitals signs and details of the injury.

Donna Waddle, crying, clutched Brett's hand. Each time she looked at her son's face, she would cry even more. The swelling was now so rapid that Brett's right eye was completely swollen shut. It didn't seem possible to Larry Waddle that his son's head could swell any farther without bursting wide open. A mental picture of that happening forced him to look away, tears streaming down his face.

For the Waddles, the ambulance ride seemed to be taking forever. In actuality, they arrived at the hospital emergency entrance in a little less than eight minutes. The back doors were pulled open, and the parents were quickly forced out of the way as a staff of emergency personnel had Brett out of the ambulance and into the Emergency Room within a matter of seconds.

Inside, two doctors began a quick evaluation of the damage to the boy's head, while the badly shaken parents watched from across the room. Then came the words from one of the doctors that Donna had feared the worst. "Get the neurosurgeon in here, Stat! Then prepare operating room one for immediate surgery."

The Emergency Room erupted in a flurry of activity with the Waddles caught up in the middle of it all. Turning to her husband, Donna nearly collapsed into his arms. "God, Larry, we're going to lose our boy!" she cried. "He's going to die, isn't he?"

Larry Waddle's lips quivered as he fought to keep from breaking down himself. Stroking Donna's head as gently as possible and holding her tight to him, he tried to reassure her that everything was going to be all right. They had a great hospital and great doctors working on Brett.

"He's going to make it, darling. You'll see. He's a tough kid," he whispered.

One of the nurses took Larry's arm and led the couple down the hall to a waiting room.

"Please wait here," she said. "We'll keep you updated on your son's condition."

For a few minutes, the Waddles found themselves alone. Neither spoke, each silently praying that the other was strong enough to bear the burden of this awful night should things not go well. The solitude was soon interrupted by a flood of friends and neighbors who had just arrived from the ballfield. Donna's parents were the first to hug her and tell her everything would work out, she just had to have faith. The next person to approach her was Mickey Roman, the star batter and catcher for the Outlaws. It was his bat that had done the damage. With tears welling up in his eyes, he tried to find the words to say how sorry he was about what had happened. Donna could tell by the look on his face that the boy was about to break down any moment.

Reaching out for him with open arms, she gave him the reassurance he so desperately needed. Hugging him close to her, she whispered, "I know, son, I know. It wasn't your fault. Don't blame yourself. We don't."

Within the hour, the waiting room was filled to capacity, and small groups of people lined the hallways, all waiting for word on Brett's condition. Another welcome arrival was Pastor Robert Cummings, who provided a much-needed feeling of comfort and security for the

Waddle family. As he sought to comfort Donna, a nurse appeared at the door.

"Mr. and Mrs. Waddle, the doctor needs to see you now. If you'll please follow me."

A hush fell over the room as the couple nervously followed the nurse down the hallway to the waiting elevator. Donna wanted to ask a hundred questions while the elevator rose to the fourth floor, but she was equally afraid to ask a single question, for fear of what the answer might be.

Dr. Paul Turner was waiting for them outside the operating room. The expression on his face was anything but hopeful. Larry could feel Donna's hand trembling. Both expected the worst. Directing them to a small conference room next to the surgical unit, Dr. Turner asked them to sit down. He sat on a coffee table directly in front of the couple. Larry could tell the man was carefully planning what he was about to say.

The young doctor sat there in silence for a moment. He wanted to be honest about the situation but break the news to them in as thoughtful and as compassionate a way as possible. Unfortunately, there was no easy way to prepare them for what he was about to say.

"Larry, Donna. Brett sustained a skull fracture to the right side of the head. Luckily, he was brought in early enough for us to operate immediately. We've gone in and repaired the damage. The speed with which this was accomplished is a plus for our side. There is still considerable swelling, but we have taken steps to alleviate that problem. I fully expect the swelling to begin receding within the next seventy-two hours."

"Then there's no brain damage. Is that right, Doctor?" asked Larry.

"No, Larry. I believe we're fine in that area. But . . ."

The momentary relief the couple had experienced suddenly disappeared. "But what, Doctor?" asked Donna, tightening her grip on Larry's hand.

Dr. Turner shifted uncomfortably on the table. There was no easy way to put this. "Brett received a terrific blunt trauma, not only to the side of his head, but to his eye as well. I'm afraid the blow tore the iris and ruptured the sclera—the white of the eye. This caused severe damage and I'm afraid . . . permanent blindness to his right eye."

Donna could not restrain herself any longer. She broke into tears.

While Larry struggled to remain strong and comfort his wife, the doctor, excused himself. He had to go to intensive care and check on Brett's condition. Standing in the doorway, Dr. Turner wanted to offer them some slim thread of hope, but he had seen firsthand the damage done to the eye, and in his professional opinion that hope just wasn't there.

Seeing Pastor Cummings in the hallway, Dr. Turner suggested that now would be a good time for him to go to the Waddles. Within minutes the pastor was with the couple. They talked for a moment, then joined hands and prayed for Brett.

In the waiting room and down the hallway, word spread quickly about the young pitcher's condition. No one took the news as hard as Mickey Roman. With tears streaming down his cheeks, he asked the Outlaws' coach to lead the team to the chapel. He wanted them to pray for Brett. He felt that his single prayer alone would not be enough. Maybe if they all prayed together, God would have a better chance of hearing his plea. It was a proud coach that led his team to the chapel that night, where they remained for two hours.

That Sunday, churches throughout the area offered up prayers for young Brett Waddle. Mickey Roman, his parents, and a large number of the Outlaws returned to the hospital chapel every night to pray for Brett. It seemed everyone in town was pulling for the young pitcher the only way they knew—through prayer.

By the fifth day, Dr. Turner had contacted a top eye surgeon in Boston, who agreed to come to Omaha to examine Brett as soon as the swelling had gone down. After a week had passed, Dr. Turner contacted Boston again. The swelling had subsided considerably, and Brett was fully conscious. Dr. Ehrlick assured him that he would be in Omaha the following day.

That night, the Waddles, Donna's parents, Mickey Roman, and Pastor Cummings stood at Brett's bedside and prayed together as the pastor read passages from the Bible about the healing wonders performed by Jesus Christ, chief among those, healing the blind.

The following afternoon, Dr. Ehrlick arrived. After going over the X rays and Brett's medical charts, the two doctors arrived at Brett's room to find the group from the night before once again praying as they waited for the doctors. Brett was awake, and other than a slight headache, he said that he felt better than he had the last few days. But he was wor(ried about his eye. He hoped that Dr. Ehrlick could do something for him.

Everyone moved to one corner of the room to allow the doctors and nurses room to work. Slowly the bandages were removed from Brett's right eye. There was still a lot of bruising, but the swelling had definitely gone down considerably. Leaning over the boy, Dr. Ehrlick began his examination. After only a few minutes, he whispered something to Dr. Turner, who then leaned forward and studied

Brett's eye. The people across the room could not hear what was being said, but they could tell something was going on.

A nurse left the room suddenly and returned with a portable ophthalmoscope (a slit lamp microscope). Dr. Ehrlick had the blinds closed and the overhead lights turned off. He then turned on the scope. Its brilliant illumination and lens magnification allowed the specialist to examine each part of the eye meticulously.

At one point, Dr. Ehrlick had Dr. Turner step forward and look through the lens. Then he had the lights turned on again. As the nurses removed the scope, Dr. Turner motioned those in the room over to Brett's bed, while Dr. Ehrlick removed an eye chart from his briefcase.

Dr. Turner slowly shook his head as he said, "I don't have any explanation for what you are about to witness." He went on to explain that Brett's eye had been so damaged when he first saw it in the operating room that by rights the boy should be blind in that eye. The swelling had been so bad that Dr. Ehrlick would not have been able to perform surgery for at least a week, yet the torn iris had been repaired somehow. There was only the slightest trace of a fine-line scar where the tear had been and absolutely no sign that a ruptured sclera had ever occurred. In fact, other than the bruising and the slight scarring of the iris, Brett's eye was as perfect as anyone's in that room.

"Praise the Lord," said Pastor Cummings. "He has heard our prayers."

A series of Amens came from everyone, especially from Mickey Roman, who, with tears streaming down his face, managed an emotional, "Thank you, Jesus! Thank you!"

Dr. Ehrlick then placed a card over Brett's left eye and held the eye chart up in front of the boy. Brett read every letter perfectly with his right eye. Moving to the end of the bed, the doctor repeated the test, Brett again reading every letter without a single mistake. When he accomplished the same feat with Dr. Ehrlick holding the card in the doorway, everyone in the room, including the doctors, realized that they had witnessed the silent work of the Great Physician himself.

One year later, another examination revealed that the slight scar that had been on the iris had completely disappeared.

Today Brett Waddle is pitching baseballs with pinpoint precision for a top-ranked college in the midwest, where he has been heralded as a future star of a big-league team, and he will become one of the "boys of summer" soon after graduation.

As to the medical reasons for Brett's recovery, both doctors agree: You need not go any farther than your own Bible. . . .

## DARRIN'S WALK

A handsome young man walked proudly into the Children's Hospital in Tulsa, Oklahoma. He was there for an appointment with a well-known doctor. This was a momentous occasion in his life, for he was going to take his physical before entrance into the United States Air Force.

The doctor performing this physical was the physician who had treated him when he had been afflicted with Perthes' disease at the age of nine.

Darrin Shaw's parents will never forget that year, when he, the eldest of three sons, had just turned nine.

On the day after Christmas 1983, Mrs. Shaw had gone into town to take advantage of the after-Christmas sales. She left Darrin and his younger brothers in the care of a sixteen-year-old boy, who had often watched them in the past when she needed to be away a few hours.

When she got home late that afternoon, the boys greeted her in their usual high spirits and prattled away about the fun they had had with their sitter, especially about the game the sitter and Darrin had played, a sort of tug-of-war with each boy's legs tied with a strap.

Whether this was responsible for what happened, no one will ever know, but two days later, Darrin began to limp.

His mother noticed the limp one morning and asked him if he had hurt his leg. When he told her no, she didn't worry about it. Everyone knows boys continually roughhouse and engage in more than their fair share of horseplay, so Darrin's mother figured this was nothing more than a bruise.

But after three weeks went by and Darrin was still limping, his mother grew concerned, especially when she realized that the limp was getting worse. Over her son's protest, she took him to the family doctor, who promptly came to the same conclusion: It was no more than a deep bruise that should clear up on its own.

Two weeks later, however, Darrin came home from school, complaining that his left heel hurt. His mother examined the foot carefully but could not find any sign of injury.

Over the next few days, Darrin continued to complain more and more about the pain in his heel. His father noticed that his son seemed to be favoring his left foot, trying, when possible, to keep it from touching the ground when he walked. He pointed this out to his wife and reminded her that their eldest son was a pretty tough young man who hardly ever complained about anything. But it was obvious that he was walking with a great deal of pain.

Linda Shaw took him again to the family doctor, who this time ordered X rays be taken. Later that afternoon, she received a call from the doctor. There was a hint of deep concern in his voice as he explained that Darrin was a victim of Perthes' disease. As he expected, Linda Shaw had no idea what he was talking about. Just what was it?

The doctor went on to explain that this was a disease in which changes take place in the bone at the head of the femur that result in deformity. He urged her to make an immediate appointment with an orthopedist at the Children's Hospital.

Within a few days, Darrin and his mother were sitting in the specialist's office.

The physician examined Darrin carefully and then called in another orthopedist for consultation. They compared notes then told Linda that her son should be admitted to the hospital as soon as possible. They pointed out something that she had not noticed before—that Darrin's left leg was underdeveloped compared with the right and was already a good one and a half inches shorter.

During the ten days that the boy was in the hospital, more X rays were taken. The diagnosis was confirmed beyond any doubt, and Darrin was placed in traction. This had no effect on the left leg, so he was then placed in a cast from his chest to his toes and released from the hospital.

This was in February. Four months later, in June, he returned to the hospital, where the cast was removed and more X rays taken. He was then placed in another cast, which was to remain until August.

It was in mid-July that Linda was talking with a neighbor about Darrin and his condition. The neighbor asked, "Have you ever thought of contacting the Prayer Tower at Oral Roberts University and having them pray for Darrin?"

Linda was beside herself. Why hadn't she thought of that? The world-famous evangelist lived in Tulsa, and the university that he had established though his ministry was less than a mile from her home. Although she had never attended a service there, she had heard of some of the amazing events that often occurred at those services. That very afternoon she phoned the Prayer Tower and asked that Darrin's name be included with the hundreds of others they received every day.

The first week in August, Linda took her son back for X rays. The cast was removed, and he was given a brace instead. It had been hard enough to be in a cast during the blistering heat of that summer, but the brace, which extended from the boy's hips to his toes and weighed fifteen pounds, proved even more uncomfortable. Darrin, extremely patient during this whole period and never complaining, now pleaded with his mother, "Mommy, please, can't I have the cast back instead of this brace?"

This plea broke Linda's heart, particularly in view of the fact that in all likelihood he would have to wear such a brace for the rest of his life and that his leg, unless touched by God, would more than likely grow progressively worse, continuing to become shriveled and deformed.

Linda called in a prayer request to the university every week, and in the last week of August, she attended her first service at Oral Roberts University. As she entered, she felt something in that auditorium she had never felt before. Linda couldn't explain it, but she knew she wanted to go back.

The following week, Linda took Darrin with her to the services, brace and all. Other people that day were wonderfully healed, but not Darrin. But Linda did not lose faith. They continued to attend the services regularly.

When Linda and Darrin arrived at the auditorium, the first week in October, they were a little late that day and could not find a seat, so they stood back against the far wall as the services got under way. When they came to the part of the service that offered prayer for the afflicted, Linda noticed that Darrin's leg began to twitch. In that instant, Linda knew that the power of God was going through her son's leg.

Looking at her son, Linda saw radiance in his young face. She held him close and began to cry. Then she suddenly realized that what remained to be done now was between her and God. She would have to have the faith to believe God to the point of action—her action. She said a quick prayer, and before it was finished, she knew she had been given the faith.

With her son's hand in hers, Linda took him to the ladies' lounge. She told him to wait there for a moment, and she went to find an usher. She asked the first one she saw to get her a screwdriver. The young man managed to find one rather quickly for her. Thanking him, she returned to the lounge.

There was a prayer on her lips as she took the screws from the brace and removed it from her son's built-up left shoe. She then had Darrin take off both shoes and told him to walk across the lounge. He did so without difficulty and without the slightest sign of a limp. Linda then stood him before her and quickly saw what had happened: The left leg had miraculously lengthened and was exactly the same as the right!

When they left the campus of the university, Linda was carrying Darrin's brace with her.

The following morning, she called the doctor and told him she had removed the brace. The doctor was horrified to hear what she had done. He quickly told her that removing the brace would do incalculable damage, taking from the boy any hope of future improvement.

Linda was terrified that he was right, and during the next few weeks she was torn by the most terrible doubts she had ever endured. She had acted in and by faith. She completely believed in the power of God to heal; she knew God had touched Darrin. But then, she told herself, God works through doctors as well. Perhaps she should pay attention to what the doctors were telling her.

During those next few weeks she put the brace on and took it off a hundred times. After talking with the doctors, she would replace it, and after earnest prayer, she would take it off.

One day, almost immediately after she had put it back on, the leg broke out in boils. Today Linda believes this was God's way of speaking to her, but at the time she was too upset and uncertain to realize that.

She took it off then until the boils went away, and then put it back on. This time the leg almost at once and for no discernible reason turned black and blue. That was enough proof for Linda. This truly had to be God's way of telling her to set aside her fears and believe.

Darrin's leg, from the moment his mother first took the brace off at the Oral Roberts University, has remained perfect.

At the request of his doctors, Linda took Darrin back at regular intervals for checkups. They were astonished by his healing and conceded that there was no known medical explanation for what had happened to him. They concluded that it was, as Linda said, a miracle.

In 1987, Linda received what is one of her most prized possessions: a letter dated March 1985, signed by both orthopedists who had treated her son. They asked that she bring Darrin back to the hospital and offered to pay any expenses involved so that he might help others without faith to believe and prove to them the healing power of God was real. The Shaws donated the brace that their son had worn before his healing to the hospital.

Darrin went on to attend Oklahoma University, where he played baseball and proved to be an outstanding basketball player as well. After graduating, he chose to join the United States Air Force. But before the air force would accept him, it had him return to the doctors who treated him for Perthes' disease and had them perform the required physical for acceptance into the military forces of the United States.

Darrin passed with flying colors and is now an officer in the United States Air Force and a top-notch combat fighter pilot.

## RYAN'S STORY

Charles and Patsy Behan are more than willing to discuss the power of healing prayer with anyone who may have doubts about God's awesome power. You see, they have firsthand knowledge of that power.

Before moving to Oklahoma, the Behans had spent their entire lives in the little town of Briarville, Kentucky. Charles worked as a shift foreman at one of the mines, and Patsy taught school.

Briarville wasn't a very big town; some wondered if you could call it a town at all. And in a town with a population of fewer than one hundred people, it goes without saying that everyone knew everyone else. But for a lot of people it was just the right size. Whenever there was a problem in the town, everyone pitched in to help out, whether it was to replace the roof of the church or to help John Mitchell build an addition onto the back of his general store. Everyone pitched in and did his or her share of the work. If someone came down with the flu or some other illness, the ladies of the town would gather at that person's home and fix the meals for the rest of the family, do the laundry, and help with the kids.

There were twenty-three children in the school. There was a general store, one filling station with a single gas pump, a recreation building used for social events such as dances, bingo, and the once-a-month town meetings. The nearest hospital was a hundred miles west in Lexington. But the town did have a doctor. Her name was Martha Carpenter. She was sixty-five years old but still spry as a young chicken and sharp as a tack when it came to tending to the medical needs of her community. She had delivered practically every baby born in the town and in some cases second and even third generations. And of course, there was the church and Reverend Paul Underwood, who tended to the spiritual needs of the people of Briarville. The one thing the reverend could count on was a packed house every Sunday.

The normal calm of this quiet little community was shattered on the morning of April 9, 1993, when the residents woke to find the skies dark and threatening. There was a strange stillness in the air, and the humidity was so thick you could have cut it with a knife. Charles and Patsy stood on the front porch and surveyed the blackened sky, all the time trying to mask their concerns from their nine-year-old son, Ryan, who had no way of knowing that conditions on this particular morning were ideal for spawning a tornado at any moment.

Few residents of Briarville had their own storm cellar. Whenever the weather became threatening, everyone went to the church basement, which provided plenty of space and considerable safety. Charles and his wife could feel the change in the air as the clouds began to slowly twist in on themselves and to slowly rotate. From down the road, Mrs. Brown, their closest neighbor, yelled for them to head for the church. There was no doubt about what was happening directly overhead.

Grabbing a few things from the closet, the Behans took Ryan's hand and began to walk toward the church just as the first few raindrops began to fall. Up along the ridges of the mountains that surrounded Briarville, a series of bright flashes danced, followed by a terrific crack of thunder. The sky was going to open up at any minute with a torrent of rain.

For some reason (Patsy now believes it was because of the bright flashing of the lightning) Ryan suddenly stopped in the middle of the street. He was no longer holding his mother's and father's hands, and they walked twenty to thirty feet before they realized he was no longer with them.

Patsy Behan will never forget what happened when she turned to yell for her son to hurry along. One moment Ryan was standing there looking up at the sky, then, in the blink of an eye, a bolt of lightning came straight down and seemed to consume her young son in its bright, blinding light.

The impact of the energy from the strike was so powerful that it knocked both Charles and Patsy off their feet. When they looked up, they saw little Ryan lying in the street. He was not moving, and his clothes were smoldering. A cry of anguish came from both parents as they ran to their son, certain that he was dead. They were soon joined by others from the church who had witnessed the terrible event.

Remarkably, the boy still had a pulse, but his breathing was almost nonexistent. The soles of his shoes had been blown out, and his feet and hair were badly burned, but he was alive. As they picked up his small body, the skies broke open, and they suddenly found themselves being battered by heavy rain and powerful winds. Rushing to the church, they called for the doctor as they raced down the steps into the cellar.

Dr. Carpenter directed them to place Ryan on a long table against the wall, and she immediately began to examine him.

"Oh, the poor little dear," said the doctor as she looked at his feet. "He's unconscious and in shock," she continued. Checking his head, she saw blood trickling from both of his ears and found a small trace of blood in his nose. Shaking her head, she whispered, "Oh, this is not good. We have to get him to Lexington right away."

One of the men from the mine shouted from near the door, "You can forget that, Doc. A rain this hard will flood out the main bridge. No way we can get out of here till it stops raining and the river goes down."

Patsy had known Martha Carpenter all her life. She had delivered Ryan. In all that time, Patsy had never seen the doctor express such a look of hopelessness. There was nothing she could do.

Falling to her knees next to the table and holding her son's hand, Patsy began to cry and beg God to spare her son. Charles, still stunned by the realization of what had happened, looked to the doctor for help. She could only shake her head sadly.

"I'm sorry, Charles, but there's nothing I can do. I'm afraid he won't last very long. He has severe trauma, and his eardrums are shattered. There's just nothing I can do."

The room was silent for a long moment. The people of Briarville wiped tears from their eyes as they stared blankly at the floor. They were losing one of their own, and such a young one at that.

The silence was broken by the strong voice of Reverend Underwood, who bellowed, "Well, Martha, if you ain't got the power, then we know who does, don't we folks?"

As realization of what the reverend had just said began to sink in, the townspeople gathered around the table and went down on their knees, Dr. Carpenter included.

For the next two hours, while a howling storm roared all around them, the people of Briarville, Kentucky, prayed—as they had never prayed before—for the life of a small boy. By the end of the third hour, the storm had begun to subside, but the praying continued.

Reverend Underwood finally stood, tears filling his eyes, when he saw the small hand clasped so tightly by Ryan's mother slowly begin to move. Patsy screamed with joy as she realized her son was moving. Leaping to her feet, she began to hug and kiss him. Ryan's eyes were open.

Dr. Carpenter pushed her way to the table and quickly examined him again. His eyes were wide open and appeared normal. His pulse and heart rate were also normal. Stepping back, she ran her hand over his small face and asked, "How do you feel, Ryan?"

There was silence in the room while everyone waited to see if the boy had heard her question.

"Fine, Doctor Martha, just a little tired. And how are you?" he asked with a smile that nearly broke Martha's heart.

Everyone in the room was crying. They watched Ryan sit up, hop off the table, and walk across the room. "Gee," he said, "why is everybody crying? Did the storm blow down the town or something?"

Young Ryan has no memory of what happened to him. But his parents and the town of Briarville will never forget. For on a stormy day in April of 1993, they witnessed the power of God delivered through the healing power of prayer.

# A GRANDMOTHER'S CHALLENGE

While working on this book, I received a call from a woman in Oklahoma City. Her name was Martha Wisler. She was calling in response to an advertisement that I had placed in a number of church bulletins, requesting that anyone who felt they had witnessed the power of God's work through prayer in the medical healing of a relative or friend please contact me.

Martha and I talked on the phone for a while that night, and I found her story so interesting that I asked if she would mind if I came to Oklahoma City to conduct a personal interview. She was most kind, and we arranged to meet that weekend. The following story is the result of that interview.

Martha Wisler is a charming lady in her late sixties. Her hair is a stunning silver, her eyes sky-blue, and her kindness and manner such that she might be considered the envy of the entire South.

Martha was born and raised in Oklahoma, where she raised three daughters and four sons. Although times were often hard, she and her husband, Earl, provided a loving home and a Christian upbringing for the Wisler children. Martha's faith was severely tested in 1952, when Earl, who had been drafted, was killed in Korea. Left alone to raise the children, her faith never wavered, and she found solace in the love she shared with her children.

Her faith would be tested again not once, but twice in 1968 and again in 1971, when her two eldest sons, both career military men, were killed in Vietnam. It was a sad time for the Wislers, but Martha held everyone together with her loving heart and strong faith in God.

She considered the fate of Earl and her two sons God's will. She believed that as much as she had loved and needed them, God had needed them more. Not a day has gone by that she has not mentioned them in her prayers.

On a warm summer day in June of 1995, Martha received a call from her daughter, Sharon. Sharon's son Kevin had followed in his father's footsteps and had chosen the military as a career. Kevin was twenty-five and a sergeant during the Gulf War. When he returned home in 1992, Sharon noticed that Kevin wasn't looking well. He seemed pale, and it was obvious he was losing weight.

When asked about this, Kevin brushed it off as nothing more than the change in climate from the Middle East to Oklahoma. But he couldn't fool his grandmother. Martha saw the difference in her grandson immediately. Her daughter was right. He was pale and underweight. That combined with the fact that he seemed tired all the time sent a warning signal to Martha. Something was wrong with Kevin, whether he wanted to admit it or not. Using her grandmotherly charms, she persuaded him to go to her doctor for some tests. Sharon's call that day was to inform her mother of the results of those tests. It was a call that would again test Martha Wisler's faith.

Sharon went to pieces on the phone when she told her mother the news. Kevin had leukemia, and it was spreading rapidly. He would have to begin treatments immediately, and even then the doctors felt it would be a losing battle.

Martha fought back the grief that shot through her very soul at hearing the news, but she knew she would have to be strong not only for her daughter, but for the entire family. If they saw her, the rock, break down, what hope was there?

Over the next few weeks, Kevin underwent chemotherapy. He did not respond to the treatments well. They wreaked havoc upon the young soldier. Hemorrhaging and acute pain racked him almost daily, but worst of all, the treatments seemed to be having absolutely no effect on the disease. By the end of the eleventh week, the doctors had given up all hope and informed the family that they did not expect Kevin to live through the weekend.

Martha had gone to her church within days of Kevin entering the hospital. The pastor and the congregation had been conducting weekly prayer services for Kevin in the firm belief that the young soldier would be healed. But now eleven weeks had gone by, and Kevin's body was slowly, painfully withering away. Doctors gave him no chance, and the rest of the family was bracing itself for the inevitable. But not Martha. She may not have been able to do anything for Earl in Korea or her two sons in Vietnam, but her beloved grandson lay only a few feet from her, and this time she was determined not only to test her own faith, but to challenge her God as well, to challenge his own words: "If ye have true faith in me, so shall ye be rewarded."

Martha asked her pastor to come to Kevin's room that night to join family members gathered around the bed. Holding hands, they each took turns saying a prayer over Kevin's thin body, touching him as they prayed. The prayers continued throughout the night, lasting until daylight. Kevin had been fading in and out all night, sometimes hearing the voices as if they were coming from far away.

It was not until sunlight was filtering into the room and Martha was saying the final prayer that Kevin's eyes opened wide and he cried that there was a burning sensation spreading through his entire body. He then began to cry uncontrollably.

"What is it, Kevin?" cried out Martha, clutching her grandson's hand. "Should I call the nurse?"

Kevin couldn't speak for a moment, then, with tears streaming down his face, he spoke clearly for all to hear. "Jesus was just here. He touched me!"

Everyone in the room was crying when the team of doctors entered the room. The nurse had already told them what had happened. But the doctors were more than a little skeptical and told everyone that they shouldn't really get their hopes up. Although even they had to admit that Kevin looked better that morning than he had since he had been admitted.

Running everyone out of the room, the doctors extracted bone marrow from their patient then sent the samples to the lab for immediate testing. The doctors suggested that everybody should go home and get some rest. But none of the family nor the pastor was going to leave that hospital until they knew the results of the tests.

As they prayed for and believed, the tests came back normal. There was no sign of cancerous cells. Three more samples and tests proved the same. There was not a cancerous cell in Kevin Wisler's body.

The medical profession says that leukemia is never healed, that it only goes into remission. But you will have a hard time convincing the Wisler family of that.

Today Kevin is no longer in the military. Medically discharged (the military agrees with the medical personnel that the leukemia is only in remission), he is as healthy and active as any young man approaching thirty. He will be married by the time this book is published.

Martha feels that God rewarded her prayers for Kevin in exchange for the true faith that she had shown in him over her lifetime.

## RALPH'S STORY

Ralph Malone of Denison, Texas, struggled to the open trunk of his car carrying three suitcases and an overnight bag. It was the final day of the family's vacation on the beaches of Galveston. It had been a great week for his wife and daughter, filled with sight-seeing, swimming, and playing along the sandy beaches, but now it was time to head for home and prepare for the following week's nine-to-five grind.

Ralph's wife, Linda, came to the door of the oceanfront motel where they had spent the week and shouted to her husband, "Ralph, have you got my makeup bag?"

Out of breath and having gained a new respect for the hardships of pack mules, Ralph dropped the pile of bags at the rear of the car and replied, "More than likely. Let me check the trunk."

While her husband searched through the bags at the rear of the car, Linda leaned against the doorway. As she waited, she noticed a group of teenage boys at the end of the parking lot. They were all laughing and piling into an old pickup truck. She especially noticed that they all had beer bottles in their hands, even the driver, who revved up the truck and, with a wild yell, sped down the length of the parking lot, clouds of smoke coming from his tires. Linda felt a stunned fear grip her very soul as she watched the truck weave from side to side and pick up speed. In an instant she saw what was going to happen, but before she could scream a warning to Ralph, her husband stepped back from the trunk of the car and into the path of the oncoming truck.

The impact tossed Ralph onto the hood of the vehicle and into the windshield. Linda heard the sickening sound of her husband's head smashing into the glass, but fortunately the glass did not shatter. Startled, the driver suddenly slammed on his brakes, sending Ralph flying off the hood. He was propelled onto the asphalt, where he rolled and tumbled more than sixty feet before his battered body came to rest near the front tires of another car in the parking lot. Still conscious, Ralph was trying to grasp what had happened, but there was nothing registering except a terrible pain that seemed to encompass his entire body.

When Linda and her daughter arrived at his side, there was no movement, and they feared that Ralph was dead. A crowd had quickly gathered as Linda knelt down next to her husband. From somewhere in the darkness of his pain Ralph could hear someone saying that he had a compound fracture of his right leg. The bone was broken and exposed, and it was bleeding considerably.

Linda pleaded for help. A young man came forward and applied pressure to slow the flow of blood while they waited for the ambulance, which was already on its way. In those long, painful minutes of waiting, Ralph felt a sudden closeness to God. An elderly woman who had witnessed the accident knelt down next to him and asked if there was anything she could do. Through clenched teeth, Ralph asked her to pray for him. Placing her hand on his shoulder, the woman began to pray for the easing of his pain and a full recovery.

In the background, Ralph could hear his wife crying and then heard his daughter clearly say, "Don't cry, Mama. Daddy is going to be all right. I just spoke to God and he told me so."

Silently, Ralph whispered to himself, "Jesus is with me and I will be all right."

Within moments, the pain began to subside, and a deep sense of peace settled over Ralph Malone.

*I am in good hands—God's hands,* he thought

to himself, and although his leg was mangled and still bleeding, the pain was gone.

In the ambulance on the way to the hospital, Linda and her husband recited the Lord's Prayer together. The doctors were waiting for them when they arrived and rushed Ralph into the Emergency Room. The fractured bone had severed an artery, and that had caused the massive loss of blood. It took more than one hundred and fifty stitches to close the gash in his leg.

While the doctors were working on him, a pastor from Saint Vincent's church happened to be in the hall. Hearing what had happened from one of the nurses, the pastor came into the room, introduced himself, then, holding Linda's and Ralph's hands, began to pray. The peace that Ralph had felt earlier returned.

But Ralph's troubles were far from over. X rays revealed that he had a skull fracture and internal bleeding as well. The doctors told him that they would have no choice but to operate the following day. One doctor suggested that they operate that afternoon, but he was overruled. Ralph's body had received a severe traumatic shock. Other doctors thought it best to wait twenty-four hours.

The following morning the pastor and a few members of his church came by. Although already under the influence of the pre-op painkiller, Ralph heard the familiar prayer he often repeated on Sundays, beseeching the merciful Father to "grant that, by merits and death of thy Son Jesus Christ, and through faith in his blood, we and all thy whole Church, may obtain remission of our sins, and all other benefits of his passion."

Ralph cannot explain what happened next, but to him it felt as if something mystical, almost supernatural, took place as he took the bread.

The priest continued to read from the Book of Common Prayer: "The body of our Lord Jesus Christ, which was given for thee, preserve thy body and soul unto everlasting life. Take and eat this in remembrance that Christ died for thee and feed on him in thy heart by faith, with thanksgiving."

He then administered the wine and continued to read: "The Blood of our Lord Jesus Christ, which was shed for thee, preserve thy body and soul unto everlasting life. Drink this in remembrance that Christ's blood was shed for thee and be thankful."

It was at the conclusion of this service, Ralph says, that he felt the healing touch of the Lord and knew that the Holy Spirit was wrapped around him. At that instant, he knew he was healed.

When his doctors came into the room again, both Linda and Ralph requested a reevaluation of his earlier tests. The doctors felt that both were unnecessarily worried about the operation, but if it would ease their concerns, they would do another set of tests. The operation was pushed back a few hours while new X rays were taken. By noon, the team of doctors were back in the room with the film in their hands. They could not explain it, but the internal bleeding had stopped. The X rays of the skull failed to show any sign of the skull fracture that had been so easily identifiable the day before.

Ralph and Linda Malone believe that the Lord's healing power began while Ralph was taking the elements of Holy Communion. Ralph was able to leave the hospital ten days later on a pair of crutches.

Today he is very active in his church. He spends considerable time visiting the sick and injured in the hospitals in his community and offers prayer for their healing.

# RESEARCH AND RECOMMENDED READING


Cornwell, John. *The Hiding Places of God*. New York: Warner Books, 1991.

Dossey, Larry. *Healing Words: The Power of Prayer and the Practice of Medicine*. San Francisco: Harper San Francisco, 1993.

Harrell, David E. Jr. *Oral Roberts: An American Life*. Bloomington: Indiana University Press, 1985.

MacNutt, Francis S. *Healing*. New York: Doubleday, 1989.